Following Jesus in the "Real World"

Discipleship for the Post-College Years

Richard Lamb

INTERVARSITY PRESS
DOWNERS GROVE, ILLINOIS 60515

InterVarsity Press® is the book-publishing division of InterVarsity Christian Fellowship®, a student movement active on campus at hundreds of universities, colleges and schools of nursing in the United States of America, and a member movement of the International Fellowship of Evangelical Students. For information about local and regional activities, write Public Relations Dept., InterVarsity Christian Fellowship, 6400 Schroeder Rd., P.O. Box 7895, Madison, WI 53707-7895.

Scripture quotations, unless otherwise noted, are from the New Revised Standard Version of the Bible, copyright 1989 by the Division of Christian Education of the National Council of the Churches of Christ in the U.S.A., and are used by permission.

Cover photograph: Michael Goss

ISBN 0-8308-1608-9

Printed in the United States of America ∞

Library of Congress Cataloging-in-Publication Data

Lamb, Richard, 1960-
    Following Jesus in the "real world": discipleship for the post-
college years/Richard Lamb.
        p.   cm.
    Includes bibliographical references (p.).
    ISBN 0-8308-1608-9
    1. College graduates—Religious life.   2. Christian life.
I. Title.
    BV4529.2.L36   1995
    248.8′4—dc20   94-45410
                                                     CIP

| 17 | 16 | 15 | 14 | 13 | 12 | 11 | 10 | 9 | 8 | 7 | 6 | 5 | 4 | 3 | 2 | 1 |
| 09 | 08 | 07 | 06 | 05 | 04 | 03 | 02 | 01 | 00 | 99 | 98 | 97 | 96 | 95 | | |

*To Lisa,
my wife and partner—
together we continue to learn
what it means to follow
Jesus in his
real world*

A Turning Point

Graduation. The "real world." Finding a job. Applications, résumés, interviews. School loans. Rent, first and last. Graduate school or work? Options and decisions, hopes and reality.

If you respond to these words with a gut reaction of anxiety, concern or confusion, then you are probably about to graduate from college, or you have recently graduated. There's reason for your feelings. If it was ever easy to graduate from college, choose a direction and move on in life, it is not easy today. The terrain is unmapped, the destination uncertain, the stakes ultimate. Life beyond college is a maze in a haze—multiple decisions, none clear-cut, each potentially a detour. If you desire to follow Jesus Christ, then in addition to the common concerns regarding graduation, you know that life involves temptation and trials. "The gate is narrow and the road is hard that leads to life, and there are few who find it" (Matthew 7:14).

How am I to pursue faith in God after college? How will my relationship with Jesus look different? Has anything I learned during my college years prepared me for the choices and decisions I face as I leave? These are fundamental questions you have probably begun to ask yourself, whether you have two months until graduation or graduated a few years ago. What does it mean to follow Jesus in the "real world"?

It helps to remember that many people have already experienced the transition to life beyond college. You face fears and concerns that are fairly common to people in this stage of life. Listen to the statements of a few Christians who recently moved beyond the college setting:

Dana: As graduation got nearer, people constantly asked me, "So, what are you doing after graduation?" This bothered me, although I expected it. At first I even thought it was cool that I had no answer or that each time someone asked I had a different answer.

Bill: My feelings as I neared graduation were mainly fears. I was afraid of looking for work, of leaving my friends and of not knowing what God wanted me to do.

Randy: I was concerned about my future when I graduated. I had no idea where I was going to live, or what kind of work would feel right, or who would even hire me.

Elisa and Dave: Our biggest concerns were probably about money. When we left on our honeymoon (immediately following graduation), we knew that when we got back we had no place to live, no jobs and no savings to speak of.

The Critical Time

Now after John was arrested, Jesus came to Galilee, proclaiming the good news of God, and saying, "The time is fulfilled, and the kingdom of God has come near; repent, and believe in the good news." (Mark 1:14-15)

Jesus began his ministry at a critical time in the life of the Jewish people. The people of Jesus' day were desperate for divine intervention in their world. They were looking for God's Messiah to come and to save them from an oppressive political reality, the Roman occupation. Jesus' very first proclamation both warns and invites his hearers to act on his timely message. The Greek word for "time" here is *kairos,* meaning "the critical time" or "the decisive point." The kingdom of God has come near, and those who hear the proclamation face a choice. The point of decision comes—and then goes. Jesus invites his hearers to respond: repent and believe the good news while there is still time.

Today there is perhaps no "critical time" or "decisive point" like that of the transition between college and postcollege. Until this point most of us were carefully prepared for almost every major educational transition. Nursery school prepared us for the fast-paced life of kindergarten; sixth grade prepared us for the increased pressure of junior high; even high school offered college prep courses and other extracurricular activities to prepare us well for college. Each had a growing variety of options. But even the wide variety of college courses, majors and activities seems pretty narrow when compared with the tremendous diversity of options for life after college: jobs, professions, graduate schools, internships, marriage and family, overseas missions, church and parachurch ministries, and the host of critical life decisions that accompany each of these choices.

Colleges do attempt to provide some aid as we make this transition—but not in ways that are especially helpful for Christians. "Faithfulness to God" is not a relevant category for most career-planning and job-placement centers at secular schools. Any help offered usually neglects considerations of faith and spiritual growth. This makes the decisive point of the transition between college and postcollege all the more critical for Christians, for we are swimming upstream as we try to make faithful choices in a faithless world.

With this appreciation of the "kairos" of the transition from college to life beyond, let's return to the initial proclamation of Jesus: the kingdom of God has come near!

Jesus invited his first hearers to join the kingdom of God. Now a kingdom requires a king. Jesus' declaration means that the King of the kingdom of God is also near. That king, as Mark spells it out, is Jesus himself. And that is the good news! If we want to respond to the kingship of Jesus, we will need to become subjects of the King by doing what he says to do: "Repent, and believe in the good news."

If you are facing graduation from college or have recently gone through this transition, you are in a "kairos" moment, a critical time, a decision point. If you understand yourself as a disciple of Jesus Christ, one who is following Jesus the King, this is a critical time to return to the basic gospel message and see how to apply it to your current experience and your choices.

This book will work toward that fundamental goal through a sequence of four steps:

☐ *examine assumptions* regarding life in the "real world"

☐ *affirm convictions* and values by which to make key decisions

☐ *identify directions* for future faithfulness based on wise discernment of God's will for your life

☐ *rekindle hope* that life beyond college can be even better than life in college and that discipleship beyond college can produce more spiritual growth, more effectiveness in ministry and a greater sense of participation in the advance of the kingdom of God.

Something That Will Last Forever

The advance of the kingdom of God—that's really what it's all about, isn't it? If you're like many people I've known, you saw dramatic evidence of the advance of the kingdom of God while you were in college. Relationships were plentiful and easily formed, so the avenues for kingdom impact were numerous. You may have seen friends become Christians. You may have helped a young Christian grow in his or her faith—or had someone help you mature in Christ. You may have taken leadership in a group—small or large—and seen God work through your willingness to take risks. My experience is that participation in the advance of the kingdom of God is addictive: once you have tasted it you want more. Perhaps the most dramatic advance of the kingdom of God you saw was in your own life, as your values and priorities changed based on a deepening relationship with Jesus Christ. If you want more, great!

The worship song "I Want to Serve the Purpose of God in My Generation" powerfully expresses this desire to participate in the advance of the kingdom: "I want to give my life for something that will last forever!" What an inspiring declaration! The song became popular partly because it verbalizes deeply rooted desires. Who doesn't want to give her life for eternally valuable goals? Who wants to give his life for trivial, mundane and temporary things?

Yet the reality is that some of the people who sang that line while in college now find themselves squandering their lives for things that can't possibly last forever. The "real world" economy just isn't hospitable to the idealistic phrasings of our worship songs. Hectic workdays yield no peace; time-squeezed relationships yield no love; materialistic acquisitiveness yields no joy. Where is the kingdom of God in all that?

I hope that you too have sung the line (at least in your heart): "I want to give my life for something that will last forever!" My hope for this book is that you may find help to get on track, get *back* on track or *stay* on track, to make choices toward that end. Jesus made a remarkable promise to his disciples in John 15:16: "You did not choose me but I chose you. And I appointed you to go and bear fruit, fruit that will last." Jesus promised that his intention in calling us to be disciples is that our lives will be fruitful. Meaningful. Effective. That our lives will make an impact. This is an amazing promise, but he said more than that. He described the fruit as "fruit that will last." Eternal fruit. Today Jesus says to us, "I chose you and appointed you to give your life for something that will last forever." There is no cause, no corporation, no movement that can promise its adherents that what they accomplish with their lives will last forever. None, that is, except the movement that Jesus proclaimed, the kingdom of God.

The desire to make an eternal impact is not a vain wish, an unrealizable, idealistic dream. Rather, it is at the very center of God's purpose for our lives. Let's settle for nothing less than Jesus' purpose for us: lasting fruit.

The Value of the Process

So let's think together about what it might look like to give our lives for something that will last forever. If Jesus appointed us to bear lasting fruit, he must have some sort of plan. That simple realization is at the heart of the critical question "What is God's will for my life?" I hope that at least a part of you is impatient and eager to know the answer to this question. (I also hope that you haven't stopped asking it and never will.) The four-step process outlined above will help to identify God's will for your life, but be patient. The *process* of receiving guidance from God is usually as important as the specific guidance received.

If you have recently graduated and find yourself still unsure of God's will for your life, then know this: you are not alone. Furthermore, God is already at work maturing you and preparing you to trust him more and more as he leads you into the future.

When I entered college I thought I had things well planned out— major, advanced study, career, the works. "What is God's will for my life?"—I thought it was clear. Now, sixteen years later, I realize that my vision for the future really had little to do with God's vision. I still don't know what I'll be doing five years from now, but at least I know that I don't know. That's fine, because I look at my life differently now. I have come to understand my life as one of "following Jesus." I appreciate the biblical phrase "following Jesus" because it expresses movement. It is a dynamic image. Since I am following Jesus and he is on the move, I am moving with him. While I am less sure about where I'll be in five years than I once was, I know that Jesus will be there. I have joined with the first disciples in responding to the invitation of Jesus to come follow him.

If you don't already see your life in this dynamic, change-welcoming way, I invite you to join with me and all those who follow Jesus. We will need to be comfortable with the process, not simply impatient to arrive. In fact, we won't arrive until we see him face to face.

1
What Do
You Expect?

When recent college graduates talk about the way life has changed
since they left college, several emotion-packed words come up repeatedly: *fear, frustration, loneliness, confusion.* It's true: the transition out
of college can be one of the most uncertain times in a person's life.
But for disciples of Jesus, this time of transition can also open up
tremendous potential for growth.

Think back to what you thought college would be like. As a high
schooler, I was pretty sure that growing as a Christian would be extremely difficult in college. In fact, Christian growth wasn't necessarily
even a concern for me—mere survival was all I was hoping for. But
soon after I arrived at college, I joined a Christian fellowship that
helped me grow more in a few years than I had in my whole prior
life as a believer. Going to a secular university proved to be not the
end of my Christian walk, nor a detour for it, but the critical path
along which much of my growth occurred.

Maybe your experience was different. Perhaps you didn't expect to find God in college, but he found you. Perhaps you even intended to leave your faith behind, but God chased after you! Or perhaps you went to a Christian college, and there God allowed you to learn of him in and out of class.

Whatever your expectations, God probably surprised you, giving you a deeper knowledge of himself than you had anticipated. Yet now, as you leave or look back on college, it can be tempting to think that this time of rapid growth in your faith is coming or has come to an abrupt end. Back to survival mode.

All of us can expect to do more than survive as Christians after college. We can expect to thrive as growing disciples of Jesus Christ. The challenges we face can be the very things that help us learn new trust in God.

The difference between seeing life in the "real world" as a *threat* and looking at it as an *opportunity* largely reflects the assumptions we carry around about what adult life is supposed to look like. College and the "American dream" are so integrally linked in our cultural heritage that huge, fairy-tale, dreamlike expectations are placed on our life beyond college: we hope to find financial security, emotional health, romantic bliss, personal freedom, self-actualization—in short, life, liberty and the pursuit of happiness. These are high stakes! The possibility of making mistakes takes on intimidating proportions. Who will save us from the paralysis that comes over us when we face life-and-death decisions with little to go on? Let's return to the beginning of the gospel.

Prepare the Way of the Lord

The word of God came to John son of Zechariah in the wilderness. He went into all the region around the Jordan, proclaiming a baptism of repentance for the forgiveness of sins, as it is written in the book of the words of the prophet Isaiah,

"The voice of one crying out in the wilderness:
'Prepare the way of the Lord, make his paths straight.
Every valley shall be filled,
    and every mountain and hill shall be made low,

and the crooked shall be made straight,
   and the rough ways made smooth;
and all flesh shall see the salvation of God.' " (Luke 3:2-6)

Because this story is familiar, it may be difficult to grasp how radical John the Baptist's preaching was. When the word of God came to him, he appeared in the wilderness, on the outskirts of a tiny outpost of the Roman Empire. He preached "a baptism of repentance for the forgiveness of sins." Jews of the day would understand all the terms in this phrase, but certainly not the way John was using them. At that time baptism was a ceremony for ritual cleansing of Gentiles who were converting to Judaism, those called "proselytes." John's Jewish hearers would have had a category for baptism, but they must have balked at its application to themselves. Why would native-born Jews need to be baptized?

Imagine someone today preaching to the citizens of my city, Boston, "None of you are real Americans! You all need to be naturalized!" Citizens of Boston wouldn't stand for that kind of talk. "What do you mean, naturalized? My family has been here for three generations [or three hundred years]!" If you were born in the United States, you don't need to be naturalized. You already have citizenship.

As with us, so with the Jews in John's time. Baptism meant more than simply taking a bath. It designated entrance into a whole new culture. God designed the Jewish culture to be different from the other nearby cultures. Baptism was a sign of the unique covenantal relationship between God and his people, the people of Israel. Through the symbolic cleansing, "unclean" Gentiles were purified and allowed to enter into this covenant relationship. But it required a total cultural change, affecting all of life: religious rituals, food, work, rest, family, morality, social patterns and allegiances.

But John took the familiar ritual of baptism and gave it new meaning. John proclaimed the coming of a new kingdom and a new citizenship. His preaching is parallel to that of Jesus in Mark 1: a kingdom is coming, and people need to be prepared to declare their allegiance to the new King. The image John uses in Luke 3:4-6 makes this clear: the King is coming, so prepare the road to welcome him.

Fill in the potholes; take out the speed bumps; smooth out the road. John's message is "Prepare for the coming King!" The question we must ask is, How? John's first hearers asked the same question . . .

Bear Fruits Worthy of Repentance

John said to the crowds that came out to be baptized by him, "You brood of vipers! Who warned you to flee from the wrath to come? Bear fruits worthy of repentance. Do not begin to say to yourselves, 'We have Abraham as our ancestor'; for I tell you, God is able from these stones to raise up children to Abraham. Even now the ax is lying at the root of the trees; every tree therefore that does not bear good fruit is cut down and thrown into the fire."

And the crowds asked him, "What then should we do?" In reply he said to them, "Whoever has two coats must share with anyone who has none; and whoever has food must do likewise." Even tax collectors came to be baptized, and they asked him, "Teacher, what should we do?" He said to them, "Collect no more than the amount prescribed for you." Soldiers also asked him, "And we, what should we do?" He said to them, "Do not extort money from anyone by threats or false accusation, and be satisfied with your wages." (Luke 3:7-14)

John must have been a fascinating man. The Gospel of Mark tells us that he dressed in the style of Elijah, the great prophet of former times. He spoke with power and conviction, drawing thousands out to the inhospitable wilderness to hear him. And what gentle words of encouragement does he have for those who have honored his preaching by their coming? "You brood of vipers! Who warned you to flee from the wrath to come?" John had a way with people, didn't he?

What is the answer to John's rhetorical question? "Who warned us to flee the wrath to come? You did, John!" So why isn't John the Baptist satisfied?

John knows his audience too well to be satisfied with record turnouts. He knows that these people have a tendency to want to justify their own lives before God because of their standing as Jews. John says to his audience, "Don't even *try* to say, 'We are children of Abraham'! Don't give me any of that!"

In the Jewish culture, being a child of Abraham would usually do it. The ability to claim the proper pedigree would have been considered enough to ensure salvation from impending judgment. Yet John changes the definition of citizenship. To be included in God's people, one must "bear fruits worthy of repentance." John wants to see people whose lives have demonstrated that they really have repented, not just people who are willing to participate in one more ritual in a religion filled with rituals.

To understand what John wants, we need to understand the difference between being a "child of Abraham" and bearing good fruit. Being a "child of Abraham" is passive and static; it is simply a state of being. And John makes it clear that bearing fruit worthy of repentance requires action, involving choices and direction.

The Jews of John's day said, "We are children of Abraham." We evangelicals are prone to make the same sorts of pronouncements: "I'm a born-again Christian." "I believe the Bible." "I *teach* the Bible!"

The Jews thought their standing before God was determined by their ethnic heritage. We can tend to think our standing before God has to do with our Christian heritage, our résumé and credentials. Not that we'd actually claim to be justified by our deeds—we can spot works theology a mile away. But deep down, we all have a tendency to think that what makes us acceptable to God is the things we have done for him that differentiate us from others who haven't been as faithful.

In response to this attitude John calls for only one thing: repentance. We must turn away, make a 180-degree turn. To prepare for the coming of the King, we must leave behind what we formerly embraced. John is talking about true, not cosmetic, change. The issue is both timely and decisive: "Even now the ax is lying at the root of the trees; every tree therefore that does not bear good fruit is cut down and thrown into the fire."

The crowd responds to John's preaching by asking, "What then shall we do?" It's a good question. John then very plainly tells them how to practice repentance. Interestingly, he focuses on relationships, daily activities and practical situations. He doesn't say, "You guys aren't religious enough! Pray more, fast, tithe and do more rituals." Instead he says, "Be just in your relationships. Care for someone in need." For John's hearers, taking up his challenge will mean severe cuts in income, privilege and power. Acting on any of John's challenges will affect people's standard of living.

We often think of repentance as what happens in prayer between us and God. It doesn't tend to cost much; it is personal and chiefly attitudinal. Here John expects an attitude change, but the actions must illustrate repentance. John challenges his hearers to respond to the coming King with costly actions at the relationship level. John addresses the issues that affect us most deeply: money, power, food, clothing—the basics.

John's role, as spelled out in the Isaiah prophecy, is to prepare the way of the Lord. John paved roads in the hearts of the people, calling them to repentance. Yet Luke tells us that John was preaching *good* news to the people (3:18). The good news is that the King of the kingdom of God is coming! We must be prepared to welcome him; we must hold this purpose in mind as we turn from the things that keep us from him. The picture in Scripture is that repentance always accompanies belief: "repent, and believe in the good news" (Mark 1:15). We must turn from the things we have trusted in so that we can embrace the coming King.

So what does repentance look like for those who are about to launch into life beyond college?

Let Go of Your Branches

Imagine that you've fallen off a cliff.

I didn't choose this image because of its similarity to the experience that is the subject of this book, but it is perhaps a fitting image. Perhaps you have had recent dreams of falling off a cliff, getting in touch with your psyche's deep fear of the unknown. Or you may have recently graduated and feel as if you already did fall off a cliff.

Imagine that you have fallen off a cliff—and are hanging on a branch. You are not going anywhere—but you can't get up. The image

I am thinking of comes from the cartoon story of Wile E. Coyote and the Road Runner. The coyote has fallen off the cliff, you think he's dropped to his death, but he proves to be holding on to the branch of a tree, which just happens to be growing out from the cliff wall. At least he's not falling—he's safe for the time being, though he's not yet on solid ground.

So here you are, hanging from a branch on the side of a treacherous cliff. A man stands at the top of the cliff. "Do you need some help?" he asks.

All you can manage to say is "Yes, please."

The man offers you his hand, but though he is quite strong he cannot rescue you until you let go of the branch. So he says, "Please, let go of the branch."

What do you do? "No, pull me up first," you plead. But you realize that he's right: you can't be saved while holding on to the branch. The man at the top begs you to let go.

Why would you refuse? You might think, *If I let go, this guy might (1) be unable to save me and let me slip out of his grasp, (2) let go of me intentionally or (3) plummet over the cliff with me.* Ultimately it is a question of trust.

This scenario illustrates the nature of repentance. All of us tend to trust certain "branches" to keep us from falling or failing in life. We may recognize that these branches aren't ideal. We know they can't save us, but they do keep us from falling.

I define a branch in this sense as anything that promises security: the approval of others, athletic success, romantic relationships, career goals and achievements, money, status, self-sufficiency, political ideology, friendships. Because these things promise security, as we trust in them we are tempted not to trust in God, or we simply don't think we have to. I am not saying that all these things are bad or wrong or sinful, but like many good things, any of them can be turned into an idol. We are tempted to trust these things for security and safety rather than putting ourselves in the sure hand of Jesus.

The cliff-hanging scenario illustrates two fundamental and simple truths: we all desperately need to be saved, and Jesus is the only means of real salvation. The only life the world has to offer us is like hanging on the edge of a cliff. No amount of financial security can save us—the branch could break at any time, we could lose our grip. No branch the world offers can help us get to the top of the cliff; only the strong and faithful grip of Jesus can do that. If Jesus is going to save us, really save us, from the only life the world has to offer, then we must let go of these branches.

In college I found a peer group, one that valued the things of the kingdom. With the help of older Christians and fellow students, I began to let go of many of the branches that I'd been clutching tenaciously. One critical branch for me was achieving success on the world's terms. Being successful itself isn't wrong, but an idolatrous pursuit of success certainly is. For me it was a branch that offered security but was ultimately unable to save me. Until I let go, this branch kept me from making certain choices to be faithful to Jesus. Later, when my girlfriend broke up with me, I was forced to let go of the romantic-relationship branch I had held on to. As painful as the breakup was, the following six months was a rich time of growth in my faith as I found myself with only Jesus as my security. Perhaps this has been your experience as well.

In one way or another we all have lost a branch, yet probably none of us have released all of our branches. And the question now is, What then shall we do as we leave college?

Entering the "Real World"

You are about to enter the *real world*. You've used and heard the phrase many times. Of course it presents a bias, as if the college culture and environment were unreal and inferior. It subtly implies that what you have learned about discipleship in college won't work after college. Others may advise you, "It's fine to be idealistic when you're in college, but when you get out in the *real world*, life isn't like that."

When some parents look at the lifestyles of collegiate Christians, they aren't especially excited. Perhaps Christian growth has involved learning to value people more than grades and material belongings.

So with your time, possessions and even money you are generous and hospitable to the people around you. Yet your parents may think, *I didn't send you to college to learn how to be kind to street people and help other people with their relationship problems.*

Your parents may well have tolerated your Christian activity and growth in college because they could comfort themselves with the thought, *At least Karl [or Kari] will still end up with a degree. Surely he/she will have enough sense to settle down and get a job, go into the real world and live a normal life.* Added to such spoken or unspoken expectations is the "wisdom" of professors and peers who remind you, "Things will all change in *the real world.*"

The fact is that many things *do* change upon graduation from college. Certain routine situations, like eating at a dining hall with a dozen friends, are no longer routine at all. Sleep patterns, work deadlines, free-time availability—all these do change, sometimes drastically.

But some more fundamental things don't change. What doesn't change is the reality of the world as described by Jesus and his call to his disciples to follow him. Jesus' authority in your life will not suddenly be invalid when you graduate.

As we Christians leave college, we face a real challenge as we reject the set of values and principles preferred by the non-Christian world. We must learn how to apply biblical convictions and values to a new set of circumstances and a different context. As we continue to grow in understanding of God's Word and in our experience of God, we expect that our convictions will mature and change. Yet the new context itself doesn't and shouldn't invalidate all we have already learned about what it means to follow Jesus.

Repenting of Assumptions

Our lives are filled with expectation and hope as we graduate from college. We send out announcements and receive cards and gifts from well-wishers who have high hopes because of the promise we have shown. In the process we tend to take in many assumptions and hopes of others that may have nothing to do with God's design for our lives.

These assumptions are not forced on us by malevolent influences but rather are ironically imposed by those who have our "best interests" in mind.

We need to repent of holding many of these assumptions and placing our security and hope for a happy future in them. This is different from saying that none of our friends' and family's assumptions are true or will come true. For example, a good many people assume that they will get married, and most of them do marry. Yet the hope of marriage can be a branch, promising a measure of relational security and happiness. Holding on to this branch may make us less available to respond to God's leading in our lives. Letting go of the branch may in fact put us in the place where we can really experience God's guidance and provision, including his provision for us in marriage. We need to repent of clutching this branch so that we can see that God is the source even of relational security.

The following three stories illustrate several of the most common assumptions regarding life in the "real world." As you read, consider the following list of topics and identify the assumptions of each:

☐ job
☐ money
☐ education
☐ housing
☐ church
☐ lifestyle
☐ friendships and marriage

Brad. Brad was a political science major in college. He wound up in a business consulting job because the company conducted its interviews on campus with a relatively well-structured job-search process. Brad had been told he would be working fifty to fifty-five hours a week, but he found he really needed to put in sixty-five to seventy-five hours in order to stay up with the other first-year interns.

He had always liked the idea of living in Chicago, where the job was located, but he didn't know anyone there. He posted an ad at a big church for a Christian rooming situation, but nothing developed soon enough, so he rented a small one-bedroom apartment for $550 a month. This seemed high to him, but so did his pretax monthly salary of $2,400.

Having been a Bible study leader in his college fellowship, Brad had expected to get involved in a church, eventually in a teaching capacity somehow. But with the work schedule he kept, he was lucky just to have the energy and time to attend church regularly. One of Brad's best friends went to China to teach English for two years, and Brad had hoped to support this ministry financially and in prayer. But seeing his first after-tax paycheck brought him up short, especially when he totaled up rent, the costs of furnishing an apartment, and school loans. Brad never made a conscious decision about tithing, but two years later he had never given regularly, either to church or to missions. Then his intern position ended, and he went on to business school.

Janet. A literature major while in college, Janet had hoped to go into publishing. But because the job market was tight, she applied to graduate school as a backup. When no job offers came, she entered a Ph.D. program in American literature at the University of Michigan in Ann Arbor. Janet had never considered living in the Midwest, but this was the best option available. Though the area had many strong churches, she found it more difficult to get to know people than it had been in her college fellowship. As far as she could tell, she was the only Christian graduate student in her department. Most of her fellow students seemed extremely hostile to Christianity.

Steve and Amy. Having dated all through college, Steve and Amy were married the weekend after graduation. She found the job she had prepared for during college, teaching junior-high school; he began work with an accounting firm. Their first year out of college was extremely difficult. Struggling to adjust to the demands of teaching, Amy gave her job a good deal of emotional energy, while Steve was working forty-five to fifty hours a week in addition to studying for the CPA licensing board examinations. They felt lucky to find an apartment halfway between their two jobs, so that each had to drive only twenty-five to forty minutes each way.

The demands of their schedule and their desire to build their young marriage left them without time for regular fellowship, apart from going to dinner occasionally with old friends from college. They were quick to tell their friends of their dissatisfaction with the church they had begun to attend, but their motivation to do anything about it faded over time.

What unstated assumptions did Brad, Janet, Steve and Amy share as they made the transition out of college?

Assumptions about jobs. Perhaps the most dangerous assumption in decisions about life after college is the unquestioned priority of finding a job over every other decision. Each of the people in the examples above made major decisions based on finding a job in a certain location. The job brought Brad to Chicago, while the lack of one sent Janet to Ann Arbor. Steve's and Amy's jobs are an hour apart by car, so that geographical fact determined the location of the suburb into which they moved.

This assumption is dangerous because it implies a relative priority of job, profession or career over church, ministry, community, friendship, spiritual growth or any other related intangibles that should be factors in our decision-making. Of course job opportunities should play a role. But in the harsh "real world" of postcollege, finding a job can too easily become the first goal. For example, the decision process used by the graduates described above followed this general pattern:

☐ Find a job, which determines a general location in which to live.

☐ Find an apartment near enough to the job.

☐ Find a solid church near to where you live.

☐ Get involved in one aspect of the church you begin to attend.

☐ Make new friends, *if possible,* in your new small group or ministry team.

But this isn't the only way to make these big decisions about life after college. Consider a group of friends and partners from a college fellowship who decided to live together after graduation and pursue ministry in an urban context together. These four friends, Laura, Suzie, Debbie and Cheryl, moved to San Francisco to pursue ministry in the Mission District, a neighborhood with a predominantly Central American population. They spent much time in prayer asking for

God's guidance. Their process was almost the reverse of the one considered above:

☐ They chose ministry partners, with whom they shared kingdom values and a common vision for life.

☐ They chose a ministry field and a church that supported and helped them to advance ministry in their field.

☐ They found an apartment in a convenient location that facilitated their ministry and relationships in their church.

☐ They found jobs that supported them while involved in ministry and in the life of their church.

Another friend made different decisions to pursue God's call on his life. Rik is a Dutch citizen who graduated from college in Boston. He hopes one day to be a self-supporting missionary in Europe. Rik speaks Dutch, German and French as well as English. In order to follow his sense of God's leading, he sought a sales job with a company that has large operations in Europe. Rik hoped for a job in Boston, where his other ministry partners and good friends were living, but he was offered a job in Hartford, Connecticut, nearly two hours away. Rik decided to take the job, and his supervisor promised that he would be transferred to Boston as soon as possible. Rik hopes to return to Europe with some of his college partners, so he has invested time to maintain his friendship and partnership with people in Boston. Recently he received the job transfer to Boston, and partnerships continue to grow.

The point is not that there is only one right decision to make or even only one right way to make these kinds of decisions. The point is that unquestioned assumptions about how these important decisions get made will be likely to dilute discipleship after college.

A second major assumption we make regarding jobs is that our identity is wrapped up in what we do for a living. After finding out a person's name, usually the next question we ask is, "What do you do?" And we don't mean "what do you do in your free time?" When we ask this question, and when we answer it, we are usually placing others (or ourselves) in value-laden boxes based on the status of our jobs. Obviously Jesus (a carpenter by trade) or the many fishermen-disciples were not hindered by working-class labels. The assumption that identity equals job has several implications:

☐ *Only certain types of employment are acceptable beyond college: full-time, professional positions with open-ended advancement potential.* In the example above, because Janet did not find such a job, she began an expensive five-year graduate program to enable her to find the kind of position she wanted. Janet's decision-making process reflected her narrow assumptions regarding acceptable employment more than it reflected hearing from God.

☐ *Your salary accurately reflects your worth to society.* This cynical attitude seeps into our thinking about ourselves and our peers. This is obviously a false economic equivalence, but the assumption is spiritually dangerous as well. How much corporate America values a certain job and how much God does are often very different.

If leaving college feels a little like jumping off a cliff, often the first branch we grab on the way down is a "secure" job. We must be willing to reconsider the decision-making process, allowing God's priorities to be reflected in our choices.

Assumptions about money. Now you have your *own* money! But it's amazing how quickly you can spend $1,500-2,000 per month even though you lived on much less while you were in school. Brad found this out the hard way after he saw his first few paychecks evaporate. He was making more than he'd expected to make, but he also wrote big checks every month and found he had to spend money on things he used to take for granted, like chairs and dishes. The sticker shock of life after college is one of the painful realities of the "real world."

My first college job involved grading problem sets for introductory calculus courses. The hourly pay was pretty good, but I only worked a few hours a week. Still, that bit of income independent from my parents gave me the opportunity to learn about generosity and tithing. I grew to enjoy spending money on other people and giving to support ministry. After graduation my monthly paycheck multiplied by a factor of ten, but at that point I was responsible for food, housing, car and living expenses. I was challenged to be generous on a larger scale, but my greater expenses tempted me to justify selfishness.

Think about your assumptions regarding your money.

☐ Do you have a budget? Do you live by it? If not, take some time now to draft a budget based on current or expected income.

☐ How much do you plan to tithe?

☐ How much do you plan to save? Remember, saving money may be a cultural value, even a wise thing to do, but it is not a right. Many families throughout the world live with no chance to save money.

☐ How is your money related to your family? Will your parents be generous with you? expect you to be financially independent? expect you to help to support them at some time in the near future?

☐ What is your strategy for paying off student loans? How do your loan payments affect how you think about the future?

One thing most of us assume regarding money is that *we will have it,* in greater quantities than we've ever seen before. Furthermore, we assume—perhaps in the face of the current economic climate—that we will have more and more money every year of our lives. Again, my point is not that we shouldn't want or have money but that it can clearly become a branch we hold on to for survival. Repentance involves honestly facing up to our assumptions and turning them over to God to open us up to his desire for our future, even and especially in the area of money.

Assumptions about education. Janet's two options were full-time work in publishing and graduate school in literature. Perhaps without any strong sense of call to academic life, she embarked on an arduous five-year (or more) journey toward the completion of a Ph.D. in American literature. Janet has bought into the common assumption that more education is better than less.

What was once enough education in many fields no longer seems enough today. Thirty years ago a B.A. degree promised success in many fields and in business. Today the emphasis has shifted to attaining master's degrees, professional degrees and doctorates.

Some Christians entering graduate studies have a keen sense of God's call and see their academic work in the context of pursuit of the kingdom of God. But it is easy to uncritically assume the necessity of graduate studies. Unless we know with confidence that God has appointed us to it, we risk wasted years pursuing something that does not yield lasting fruit (see John 15:16).

Another subtle assumption we can develop as we prepare to enter the "real world" is that it's possible to set aside some part of your life that is preparation only, *training* but not *doing*. If disciples of Jesus accept this assumption, it can lead them to relax in their pursuit of discipleship.

I know many graduates who have sensed a long-term call into medicine and have entered medical school. They are all motivated by a desire to use medical skills as a means of ministry. But medical school is an intense environment, not well suited for maintaining kingdom values. The assumption that medical school is simply a time of *preparing* for ministry and not a time to be *doing* it can slowly erode desire to serve in the name of Christ.

In contrast, Jesus prepared his disciples for a ministry of healing as he called them into it, to join him and to minister with him. Training was necessary for the first disciples, and for any disciple. But the best ministry training is always on-the-job training. Training apart from doing often leads to the trainee's undoing. (See the beginning of chapter eight, David's story, for a description of a medical student who didn't allow his rigorous medical training to keep him from participating in fruitful ministry.)

Assumptions about housing. If you haven't yet graduated from college, imagine yourself in your ideal postcollege housing. If you have graduated, try to think back to what conditions were like while you were in college. Now compare the two living situations, before and after graduation. How much space do you need? Do you have roommates? housemates? How is your space decorated? What is on the walls, floors, windows? What does the kitchen look like?

Many people would answer these questions quite differently before and after commencement. During college most of us expected to live in large dorms in cramped quarters. We expected to have roommates. But once we are out, we hope finally to live like civilized human beings! Posters and furniture that were fine for us in college are no longer adequate. We replace paper prints with framed ones, vintage

Goodwill furniture with new futons and a couch from home that still looks fine (our parents decided to pass it on and replace it with an even finer new couch).

Perhaps the most stubborn assumption regarding our housing regards roommates. Sharing a bedroom in college is OK, but after college it is almost unthinkable. Privacy is a constitutional right, isn't it? We graduate and declare, "The days of roommates are over." Over, that is, until we get married, and then we expect we won't mind so much.

I'm making a distinction here between *roommates* and *housemates*. Recent graduates looking for housing are often quite glad to share rent costs with others. Brad, in the example above, looked for a Christian rooming situation before he found his own place. He would certainly have saved rent money, perhaps paying 20 percent less to share a two-bedroom place with a housemate. But this is a far step from being willing to consider having four people live in three bedrooms, or even two people per room. The rent savings in *roommate* living situations would be substantial.

There is nothing especially holy about paying low rent, nor is there anything wrong or immoral with having your own bedroom. But "one person, one bedroom" is not the only way to live. Many people all over the world live happily without their own room. Some of us, as we set our sights on God's purposes in the world, may leave behind the assumption of a private bedroom. For, as a later chapter of this book will show, our housing choices affect our ability to seek God's kingdom and grow in our faith.

Assumptions about church. Church life can be one of the most difficult aspects of the transition out of a college-oriented fellowship group. Janet was relatively lucky as graduates go, because she found an abundance of strong churches near her in Ann Arbor. But she also found it difficult to get to know people there, and the few minutes after worship chatting with people left her feeling like a newcomer each week. She would rarely meet the same people twice. With the other three graduates whose stories I've told, she considered it important to be committed to a small group for prayer, study and mission, but neither she nor any of the others took the time to invest in such a group.

I certainly hope that active church involvement is an assumption, or a commitment, for you. But what have you envisioned as active involvement in a church? Assumptions regarding how a church operates can keep you from finding long-term satisfaction and even effectiveness in it. When you came to college, probably you didn't expect your college fellowship to be what it turned out to be. What assumptions do you have about postcollege church participation?

□ *It will be easy to find a church where I can get to know people.* Even in a church that has a strong community life, it may be difficult to get to know people. During your time in college you may have found that other students took a lot of initiative with you. The people in your church may not expect to initiate friendship with people your age.

□ *I have a lot of ideas that I want to introduce to my church.* While you have learned a lot as a Christian in college, you have a lot to learn about the church. You will need true humility to learn from those who have been committed to your church longer than you have been alive. Otherwise prepare to be shocked and humbled when you discover that people aren't necessarily immediately ready to listen to your wonderful ideas.

□ *I will find an older Christian man [or woman or couple] who will help me and disciple me.* The number of mature men and women who aren't already overbooked with church and ministry commitments is small. There are many people to learn from, but the *way* you will learn may be very different from what you have experienced in the past.

These assumptions can all lead to discouragement if the conditions they assume aren't readily found. I'm not saying that you might as well settle for a minimal existence in a mediocre church. Rather, you will have a positive church experience if you recognize the realities of church life. It makes sense to strategize for satisfying church involvement under less than ideal circumstances. If things are better than you expected, you can only be grateful. Better that than to end up like Steve and Amy in the story above, who grew dissatisfied with their own church but were too unmotivated and cynical to do anything about it.

Assumptions about lifestyle. Since the 1960s the rate of income growth in the United States has slowed dramatically. Previous generations of Americans could reasonably expect that the incomes and lifestyles of children would be half again as comfortable as those of their parents. Now economic realities are changing faster than expectations, so today's recent graduates are dealing with the shock of diminished potential while carrying unrealistic expectations.[1] For a young family of the 1990s to have what their parents had, two or three incomes are now needed where one would have sufficed in the fifties and sixties.

The current economic challenges present remarkable opportunities to people who want to be faithful disciples of Jesus Christ after college. But for this to be the case, our assumptions about postcollege lifestyle must fall under scrutiny. Culturally determined spending patterns don't take into account the priorities of the kingdom. We must ask ourselves a host of commonly unasked questions:

☐ What kind of car should I own? Should I even own a car?

☐ How will the TV and VCR be used? Should I even own a TV or VCR?

☐ What will my food budget be? Can I live without nightly Coke and pizza?

As we examine our assumptions about lifestyle, the point is not simply to choose a life as spartan and as devoid of amenity as possible. But our freedom is to make real choices regarding the luxuries of life without allowing comfort and convenience to be the overriding concerns. As disciples of Jesus we have been given a greater goal than our own immediate gratification: to seek the kingdom of God. Later in the book the topic of lifestyle will be addressed in more depth, with a discussion of kingdom motives for choosing to buy a car or a VCR as well as kingdom motives for choosing not to.

When our lifestyle is linked to seeking the kingdom of God, even choices to spend money become much more satisfying than Madison Avenue can promise.

Assumptions about friendships and marriage. College is a time for building what we hope will be lifelong friendships. The intensity of community and common experience, like a well-tilled and fertilized field, is rich soil in which friendships can flourish and grow. A Christian collegiate fellowship or a Christian college has all of this, plus the gentle rain of the Holy Spirit to nourish and deepen friendships beyond what any secular environment offers. These friends have much influence on us while in college; we often make choices about how to spend our free time, our summers and vacations, even our classes and majors, based on the influence of our friends.

But the level of relationship familiar in college is not expected beyond it: in the "real world" we are expected to make decisions on our own, without respect to the decisions, plans and influences of others. For some the operative assumption goes something like this: *Now I'm on my own. I can't let friendships get in the way of my career.*

Most of us have a deep inner sense that that is not a satisfying way to live—but we find few alternatives. We are expected to be independent of others. We are expected to let go of the past—that is part of growing up. Yet as we let go of our assumptions about our relational life after college, we may be freed to include our Christian friends and ministry partners in our plans and priorities for our future.

Of course marriage is another matter. Family members and others may actually encourage you to make decisions about finding and securing a mate. Having a bunch of unattached friends while in college is OK (although our parents are always a little worried), but once we graduate the parental and societal pressure to be linked to one partner grows strong.

God said (Genesis 2:18) that it is not good for man to be alone. This observation deeply resonates with most of us. And we may tend to assume that our need for companionship is meant to be satisfied through marriage. Yet marriage doesn't automatically happen according to the assumed timetable! In fact, for some it doesn't automatically happen at all. The divergence between our assumptions about marriage and our experience can produce resentment, anxiety and fear and can keep us from pursuing the partnership and friendship God intends for us.

Honoring Parents While Making Faithful Choices

As we tangle with the assumptions we make regarding life after college, we may recognize the great potential to disappoint our parents. Of course not everyone who takes discipleship seriously after college will face discouragement from parents. I know many students who have been empowered to make faithful choices by the support of their believing parents, and this has been true for me as well. But many people who try to go against the flow of the culture will experience tension with their parents. That is hard, because as Christians we are called to honor our parents.

Scripture gives us room to distinguish between honoring authorities and obeying them in the face of God's call.[2] It is beyond the scope of this work to address all the arguments. But one thing I know we can do to honor our parents is to communicate with them—not just our final decisions, but throughout the process.

A man once went away on a long trip, leaving his aged mother and pet cat in the care of a trusted friend. The man called his friend every night for updates to set his mind at ease regarding his loved ones. One night his friend reported that his cat had died. The man was grief-stricken, and his churning emotions led him to blame his friend: "You shouldn't have just announced that my cat died! You should have told me, 'Your cat is on the roof. I cannot get him down. I am worried about him.' Then the next night you could have said the same thing. This would have given me time to prepare for the possibility that my cat might die. Then it would have been far easier for me eventually to hear that my cat had died."

A few days later the man again called his friend, who compassionately informed him: "Your mother is on the roof. I cannot get her down."

Often, when dealing with our parents, it really does help to let them know that "the cat is on the roof." Rather than waiting until a decision is made, we can communicate our concerns, questions and leanings early in the process. If we are afraid of their objections or stipulations, their expression of disappointment or fear, the best way we can love and honor them is to communicate with them our own hopes and fears. They may or may not be able to understand, at least initially, and we may not receive their support. But over time, as we show them that it's important to us that they hear and understand the choices we make, they may grow in respect for our choices, even when they would choose differently. I have seen this process work well for many graduates, who now enjoy the full backing of parents who were once unsupportive.

                    *   *   *

Already the call to discipleship has involved letting go of the various branches to which we cling for security and safety. We have heard and responded to Jesus' challenge to let go of the things we know cannot save us. But we face many of these same choices again in the new context of life beyond college. Unfortunately, we are, at least in part, products of our Godless culture. If we don't have assumptions about life beyond college, others already have assumptions for us. Unless we stop and think hard about the choices we are making or will soon make, we will make Godless choices: not by actively rejecting Jesus, but simply by living as though God were not very relevant.

So far this book has dealt with what we are turning from. But the best part is still ahead of us: a discussion of what we are to embrace as we follow Jesus in *his real world.*

■ *For Reflection*
Entering the "Real World"
Take some time to consider how your life will change upon graduation, or reflect on the changes you have experienced since graduation.

☐ What do you expect your life to look like?
☐ What changes will (did) take place in setting and time use?
☐ What changes will (did) you experience in relationships and social patterns?
☐ What changes will (did) you experience in your lifestyle?

Repenting of Assumptions
Reflect on your own prevailing assumptions about your life when you arrive in the "real world." Also identify assumptions of people around

you, people who love you and whose opinions you value—these assumptions are likely to affect you as much as your own.

☐ Which one or two have the greatest hold on your life?

☐ What would it take to set aside these assumptions?

☐ How would you be blessed and helped to grow as a disciple of Jesus if you were to let go of these "branches" in order to cling to him alone?

Honoring Parents While Making Faithful Choices

☐ Are you making plans or weighing decisions that you have not discussed with your parents?

☐ What fears or concerns do you have regarding your parents' role in your decision-making process?

Spend some time in prayer, giving over to God your concerns and your relationship with your parents. Also spend some time thanking God for your parents, for their love and concern over many years. How could you demonstrate your gratitude and love in ways that would be meaningful to them?

2
The King
and the Kingdom

At age nine, Bich (pronounced "bick") arrived in Califoria from Vietnam with her family. Each day in her new home, Bich was painfully reminded that she was a foreigner and didn't easily fit in. Everything was new, including the language. So she applied her keen mind to learning the rules of the culture, watching those of her peers who clearly did fit in. During her early teen years she learned how to speak Californian, how to dress cool and how to act in any social situation. She made friends and began to thrive socially.

By the time Bich finished high school, she no longer had to think about how to act in each situation; she didn't need to remember the rules of her adopted culture. Bich had internalized the values of California teen society to such an extent that "native" behavior was second nature to her; her tastes, preferences and behavior were significantly aligned with those of her peers.

Bich's story illustrates something of the process of entering the kingdom of God. When we bring our lives to Jesus, he welcomes us into his kingdom. We renounce our former citizenship and become subjects of the King of the kingdom of God. But the citizenship we receive when we become Christians doesn't mean we feel at home right away in this new society and culture. As we are aware that we don't know how things operate, we respond the way Bich did, by looking around and trying to embrace the lifestyles of those who fit in.

Through study of Scripture and the work of the Holy Spirit, we first learn the *rules* of the kingdom. For some the first challenges involve not lying, not using words harshly, not fighting back and not letting one's anger flare. At the beginning we focus on rules because everything is new and we want to fit in.

But eventually the rules don't hold our attention. We no longer have to think about not lying or swearing or stealing or having premarital sex. It's not that we aren't tempted by those things, but we have internalized the rules. Increasingly the cutting edge of growth for us becomes the *values* of the kingdom—loving God and loving other people. We make positive choices to be generous, to be a servant, to honor our parents. We struggle less and less with whether to lie to someone; our struggle increasingly focuses on how best to love that person.

Finally, as citizens of the kingdom of God and as subjects of the King, we begin to embrace not only the values of the kingdom but also the *purposes* of the King. We begin to desire to "strive first for the kingdom of God and his righteousness" (Matthew 6:33). We begin to consider the implications for our own lives of the Great Commission's call to make disciples of all nations (Matthew 28:18-19). We struggle with discerning the best ways to seek and advance God's kingdom. More than simply fitting into the culture of the kingdom of God, we desire to advance God's purposes in our own lives and the lives of other people. Obviously this can take many forms, so we seek wisdom and guidance from God and others who know us.

Welcoming Christ's kingship is a process of increasingly allowing his authority and his kingdom to be the defining reality of our lives. This process takes a lifetime, and often it feels like "two steps forward,

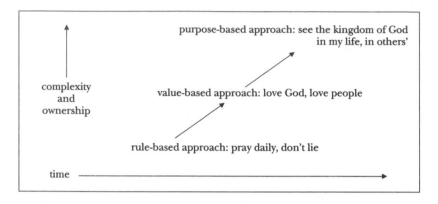

one and a half back." It isn't always an upward progression.

My expectation is that you desire to have Christ be Lord of your life and that you have experienced substantial growth in this while in college. Now the question remains, How can Christ be more fully Lord of my life as I leave college?

Leave Your Nets

Now after John was arrested, Jesus came to Galilee, proclaiming the good news of God, and saying, "The time is fulfilled, and the kingdom of God has come near; repent, and believe in the good news."

As Jesus passed along the Sea of Galilee, he saw Simon and his brother Andrew casting a net into the sea—for they were fishermen. And Jesus said to them, "Follow me and I will make you fish for people." And immediately they left their nets and followed him. As he went a little farther, he saw James son of Zebedee and his brother John, who were in their boat mending the nets. Immediately he called them; and they left their father Zebedee in the boat with the hired men, and followed him. (Mark 1:14-20)

Jesus began his ministry by preaching that people should repent and believe in order to enter the coming kingdom of God. Like John before him, Jesus preached that participation in the kingdom of God meant switching allegiances, repenting of the old loyalties and accepting the true sovereign, the King of the kingdom.

The Gospel writer Mark shows us what the desired response to Jesus' preaching looked like. One day Jesus walked by a small fishing concern on the shores of Lake Galilee. To the fishermen who worked there he said, "Follow me and I will enlarge your vision for your life. Follow me and I will redefine your purpose!" Their response was immediate and total: they left what they were doing and followed Jesus.

The Evangelist is very particular about what details he includes in this brief account. Mark fails to mention many specifics of this interaction or its prior history. This leaves the reader with a dozen questions. But he does mention a few key facts: Simon and Andrew, the fishermen, left their nets; James and John, sons of Zebedee, left their father. In each case what defined them was left behind as they became disciples of Jesus. Here we see a tangible picture of the nature of repentance and belief.

This story is familiar to us—perhaps too familiar. Think about what it would mean for a fisherman to leave behind his nets, his working capital in the only trade he had ever known. Or consider the cost to a son of a wealthy businessman to leave his father behind to work the family business alone. To Simon and Andrew, nets meant a job; a job meant security. To James and John, the family ties and family business meant relational security. Jesus' call to follow him meant to leave behind what they valued most.

Jesus' initial invitation is the same for anyone today: "Repent and believe; leave your nets and follow me." Few of us are defined by nets; few fish for a living. But all of us have netlike accoutrements defining our identity: the books of a student, the expectations of our family, dreams of success and fame. When Jesus calls us into his kingdom, he calls us to leave behind the things that had previously defined and given purpose to our lives, so that he can give us a new purpose: "I will make you fish for people." He says to us, "Follow me and I will make you into a lover of God and of people. Follow me and I will give you a role in the advancement of the kingdom of God."

This is not to say that we all must literally leave behind whatever we are doing. Yet we must not let our current activity define our identity. Some people say, "Since I am in college, I am called to be a student. That must be my top priority." This logic is persuasive for those who are not disciples of Jesus. But for us a different logic is at work: we are called first to be his disciples. So during college we may have experienced conflict between our roles as students and Jesus' call on our lives. As we leave the college setting we should expect to experience similar conflict and tension.

Of course not all Christian students struggle with overidentification with (and idolatry of) their studies. For some the "nets" are the literal nets of the basketball court, or the soccer field or the lacrosse stick. For others drama or computer games define identity. A call to follow Jesus will mean setting aside these things in some meaningful way in order to pursue a greater identification with Jesus. For a few it may even mean taking up a new, disciplined approach to academic work or graduate school, once they have set aside idolatries to respond to Jesus' call.

Lose Your Life to Gain It

He called the crowd with his disciples, and said to them, "If any want to become my followers, let them deny themselves and take up their cross and follow me. For those who want to save their life will lose it, and those who lose their life for my sake, and for the sake of the gospel, will save it. For what will it profit them to gain the whole world and forfeit their life?" (Mark 8:34-36)

These final verses of Mark 8 contain the "altar call" of the Gospel, an echo of Jesus' call to his first disciples in chapter 1. In the first half of the Gospel Jesus' name becomes well known, but his identity remains a mystery; the question repeated throughout is "Who is this man?"

Mark answers this burning question when Peter blurts out, "You are the Christ!" (see Mark 8:29). At that point Jesus begins to teach his disciples what it *means* that he is the Christ. His ministry changes gears; he focuses on the disciples, spends much less time with the crowds, heals only a couple of people and teaches repeatedly about his upcoming death and resurrection. If the question of the first half of Mark is "Who is Jesus?" the question in the second half is "What does it mean that he is the Christ?"

This then is the turning point in the ministry of Jesus. And this is when Jesus gives his altar call, his inclusive invitation for all who would follow him: "If any want to become my followers, let them deny themselves and take up their cross and follow me." If we really thought about it, we would probably wonder about Jesus' evangelistic strategy—clearly this kind of negative talk and depressing emphasis on pain and sacrifice are not the way to win friends and influence people!

Actually Jesus didn't leave his hearers with a one-sided emphasis on the cost of discipleship. He went on to give a cost-benefit analysis of the options: "For those who want to save their life will lose it, and those who lose their life for my sake, and for the sake of the gospel, will save it. For what will it profit them to gain the whole world and forfeit their life?" Here Jesus presents his logic of discipleship: The world is divided into two camps, those who lose their lives for Christ's sake and those who don't. Both groups eventually lose their lives; death is the common end. The chief difference is that one group will gain life while the other will simply forfeit it. Those in one group try to save their lives but lose them in the end; members of the other group willingly lay down their lives for the sake of the gospel, and they gain life—real life, the eternal life that begins now—in the process.

Why does Jesus say all this? Because Jesus knows that we all desire "to gain the whole world." Or perhaps not the whole world, just a parcel of prime real estate. Not worldwide fame, just the admiration of our colleagues. Not the wealth of nations, just a comfortable home with a swimming pool.

A poignant illustration of this challenge is found in the 1966 Academy Award-winning film *A Man for All Seasons*. At the end of the film, Sir Thomas More is on trial for his life. Richard, a young man Sir Thomas has known, appears as a witness and commits perjury in order to give false but deadly testimony against him. For his willingness to do this act, he has apparently been awarded the position of attorney general for Wales. As this fact becomes clear, and after all the damage has been done, Sir Thomas is saddened, not angered: "Richard, it profits not a man to gain *the whole world* and forfeit his soul . . . but for Wales?"

None of us will be given the chance to trade away our soul for the whole world, though Jesus says that it would be a bad trade anyway. Yet many willingly or unknowingly trade their souls for far less substantial recompense. Some live to regret the trade; all will die to regret it. Jesus' offer, to his first disciples and to us who would be his disciples today, is life, real life, life that does not end. In martyr Jim Elliot's paraphrase of these verses: "He is no fool who gives what he cannot keep to gain what he cannot lose."

Transition Brings Temptation

> Then he began to teach them that the Son of Man must undergo great suffering, and be rejected by the elders, the chief priests, and the scribes, and be killed, and after three days rise again. He said all this quite openly. And Peter took him aside and began to rebuke him. But turning and looking at his disciples, he rebuked Peter and said, "Get behind me, Satan! For you are setting your mind not on divine things but on human things." (Mark 8:31-33)

Jesus' response to Peter in this section of Mark 8 seems a little strong, doesn't it? As Jesus speaks about his suffering and death, Peter becomes uncomfortable. He doesn't like to hear his Lord, the Christ, speaking in such negative terms. He has a different plan for Jesus, and it doesn't involve dying. What might generously be interpreted as a forgivable excess of enthusiasm or loyalty Jesus interprets as the words of Satan! A little strong, no?

But consider what Peter is doing when he takes Jesus aside and begins to rebuke him. Jesus has been giving crucial teaching regarding his upcoming death and resurrection, which will be central to his entire purpose in coming to earth. "*No!* You can't do that!" Peter interjects. "You don't have to die. Become king! Conquer the Romans! Save your life, Jesus!"

Jesus' response to Peter's temptation emphasizes that we all must lose our lives for the gospel if we want to save them. It's as if Jesus were quoting from the rule book of the universe. He's describing something that works like gravity: If you jump out of a window, you will fall. If you save your life, you will lose it. This is true for everyone. For the crowds. For the disciples. Even for Peter, who isn't excited about following Jesus to his death. And it is true even for Jesus.

Imagine what would have happened if Jesus had listened to Peter's words "You don't have to die." This temptation from Satan would have cost him his life. And Jesus, seeing his disciples with the clarity of the only Son of God, knows that it would cost the eternal lives of all of those who would have come to believe in him.

It is no coincidence that Satan shows up at this point in Jesus' life. Jesus deals with demonic spirits a lot, but at only two other times in his earthly life does he encounter Satan and his temptation directly: in the wilderness and in the garden (Luke 4:1-13; 22:3, 40; John 13:2).

Satan shows up at key transitions in Jesus' life: the beginning of his public ministry, the point where he begins to define for his disciples the purpose of his coming, the point where he must make the final decision that seals his fate on the cross. As Jesus begins his ministry, Satan tempts him to define himself as a popular, powerful messiah and to use his power to advance his own purposes. After Jesus is revealed as the Christ, Satan tempts him again to define his Christ-hood in worldly, military terms, rejecting suffering and death. In the garden Satan's temptation is to resist death, so Jesus repeatedly prays to his Father to sustain him through it.

Satan knows that his targets are the most vulnerable to temptation at transition times. This is one of Satan's vital strategies. When we have set patterns of faithfulness and growth, it is easier to resist temptation. When we are in new situations or experiencing dramatic change in our lives, we are most susceptible to Satan's ploys.

Satan can neutralize all the progress Christians make in their spiritual growth in college if he can derail them during the transition after college. Their progress is slowed if he can persuade them that the "idealistic" convictions and choices they made in college somehow don't apply to the harsh realities of the "real world."

Satan may attack us by tempting us toward the sin of regret. We may find ourselves disappointed at the faithful choices we made in college that left us with a less-than-impressive résumé. Perhaps we gave up a prestigious summer internship to participate in a crosscultural mission; perhaps we decided not to do a senior project in order to give priority to ministry. The regret becomes a sin as we doubt God's faithfulness.

Or we may be tempted toward envy. We watch as our non-Christian roommates sail into a good job or get letters accepting them into graduate school. Our temptation may be to think that we've been left behind our peers by not getting to know all the right professors, gaining the right summer employment experience and earning the knock-'em-dead grades that would have put us into the graduate school, government post or high-tech firm of our choice. As disciples of Jesus who have internalized the values of the kingdom, maybe we only know how to love God and love other people (and when we're honest we admit we aren't always great at that either). We've been spoiled for the world, useless to a Godless and loveless society, useful only to the kingdom.

Transition into the real world is the time when Satan will be tempting us to save our lives, to change back to the rules we played by before we encountered the kingdom of God. Satan will raise doubts and questions, perhaps through the voices of others. People will belittle our experience of God's trustworthiness, and those with more worldly experience will advise us, "Now is the time to get serious—save your life while you still can."

The irony is that the strength of this temptation during the time of transition will be proportional to the degree to which we have given our lives away during college. The more we have lived by Jesus' call to lose our lives for his sake, the more we will experience a temptation to save our lives and gain our piece of the world.

We need to know that the rules we have been playing by *are* the big-league rules—this is what it really is all about. We *have* been living in the "real world," the truly real world Jesus describes. What was true for Jesus and for Peter is still true for us: we must lose our lives for Christ's sake if we want to find life. Not that it's all downhill from here:

the life Jesus promises, real life, keeps getting better and better as our discipleship deepens.

So is it really possible to continue to follow Jesus in the "real world"? Can there be continuity between discipleship during college and discipleship after college? Yes, yes, *yes!* The context for our discipleship changes, sometimes dramatically, but *the principles governing it remain the same.*

"Use the Force, Luke"

A useful and entertaining cinematic depiction of the life of discipleship is given in the character of Luke Skywalker from the Star Wars trilogy. Luke desires to become a Jedi master (a magician-warrior) like his father. Obi Wan Kenobi, "Ben," an old man who himself was once a Jedi master, encourages Luke in his quest. Luke begins training with Ben, who teaches him how to fight using "the good side of the force." (For our purposes here, let's set aside the films' pantheistic religious assumptions.)

At the climax of the first movie Luke is piloting a small spacecraft, trying to destroy the evil empire's Death Star before it is able to destroy the good guys' home base. Though an experienced pilot, Luke must struggle to use the unfamiliar targeting instruments of his craft. Just before the critical moment in his targeting run, Ben's voice comes to Luke's mind and says, "Use the force, Luke."

Luke's temptation in this new and unfamiliar situation is to abandon all that he has learned in his recent training as a Jedi warrior. Ben encourages Luke to live consistently with his training, to put away the targeting instruments used by "unbelievers" and instead rely on the guidance of "the force." And in this new context Luke does manage to resist the temptation to doubt all he has learned of "the force." The guidance of that force saves Luke's life and the lives of many others.

Luke's situation is like that of the recent college graduate who is a disciple of Jesus Christ. The newness of the experience of life in the "real world" can be disorienting; the context of life has changed, but the principles haven't. The temptation will come to question the means by which God has worked in our lives while in college and to turn elsewhere for guidance—to the technology and wisdom of society. And in these moments of temptation Jesus comes to us and says, "Heaven and earth will pass away, but my words will not pass away" (Mark 13:31). We can always rely on his words. His words are true, and to live our lives by them is the way we find life. Jesus tells us, "Use what you know. The rules haven't changed."

Context Changes, Convictions Remain

During college Anne made it a priority to spend time in prayer and personal Scripture study each day. Each semester she set up her schedule with an hour between two classes so that she could count on taking that time to pray. Anne prayed regularly in a back pew of the campus chapel; on sunny days she stationed herself on the wide chapel steps. She kept this discipline fairly faithfully for most of her junior and senior years.

After graduation Anne found a job as a paralegal in a law firm. Her job began at 8:00 a.m., and she had to leave home by 7:15 a.m. to catch a bus early enough to be on time. Anne tried to have morning prayer times, but she was a late-night person by nature. It was difficult enough to get ready for work, let alone have an hour-long quiet time, before 7:15 a.m. Anne began to try to have her "quiet times" in the not-so-peace-and-quiet of the number 70 bus route. On a good day she could read her Bible or write in her journal for an uninterrupted twenty minutes. Once a week Anne skipped lunch, walked across the street to an Episcopal church and prayed in the back pew for an hour as she had done back on campus. She often thought about the luxury of uninterrupted time she had enjoyed as an undergraduate; now her rare truly *quiet* times were deeply precious to her.

Anne's story illustrates the need for creativity to bring the convictions and priorities of discipleship into the postcollege context, to think through old lessons with new applications. This contextualization process requires perseverance as we learn to distinguish between culturally preferred values and those of the kingdom of God.

This is not to say that our convictions do not grow, deepen, develop and even change over time. What we believe about God may change as we grow to know him better. What we value and what we pursue in life may change as our wills are increasingly conformed to his will. What *shouldn't* change is our commitment to live faithfully to what we understand about God and his will for us, no matter what else changes around us.

What follows is a list of areas in which you may have developed some sense of conviction. The topics are arranged in a logical order. The first category, our relationship with God, is fundamental—it is the basis for character growth and love for others. Each successive category is built on the previous one.

Many of these categories will be discussed in depth in later chapters. Here I will simply illustrate a few of these concepts to stimulate your thinking and challenge you to take specific steps of discipleship even now.

Priority on relationship with God. Anne's story is a first example of this. But besides a personal quiet time or devotional time, a bedrock to developing a deeper relationship with God is spending time in his Word together with other Christians. During college a weekly Bible study fits easily into the pace of life. Perhaps you even led a Bible study for others or participated in a couple of small group Scripture study times each week. But after college, finding quality time for Scripture study becomes more difficult.

David, a recent graduate and relatively young Christian, told me about his upcoming financial consulting job, which would demand sixty to seventy hours a week, at least initially. David was worried that he would not have time for a weekly Bible study and feared that Sunday worship would not be enough to sustain his growth. I asked him to consider asking his manager, before he began the job, to allow him one evening each week that he could set aside consistently to attend a Bible study for twenties-age people in his church.

David was skeptical that his boss would go for it but came to believe that God wanted him to set his priorities in this way from the beginning. He spoke with his boss, explaining what his priorities were and why he needed the weekly evening off. His boss was very understand-

Relationship with God	Christian Character	Relationships with People
trust	integrity, sincerity	generosity, hospitality
seeking God in prayer	teachability, servanthood	servanthood, availability
obedience to God's will	commitment, faithfulness	forgiveness, reconciliation
listening to God through Scripture	compassion, kindness	accountability, partnership
	peace, joy	intentionality, risk-taking
		crosscultural outreach, racial reconciliation

ing and agreed to his request. So from the beginning, David's boss understood that his Christian faith was a priority in his life.

Priority on character. In college, *integrity* means not cheating. It also means not saying things you don't mean, not making promises you don't intend to keep (like "I'll call you later" or "I'll be finished with this tomorrow"). After college you have even more opportunities to cheat, whether on tax forms, expense reports or time sheets. Integrity means working diligently even when unsupervised. It may also mean quitting a job when you cannot in good conscience carry out your assigned tasks.

In college, *humility* allows us to come before Scripture ready to apply it to our lives. It produces a nondefensive appraisal of our faults and sinfulness. It also helps us forgive those who sin against us. After college we may be called upon to be a humble learner from people whom we find it hard to respect, who are quite different from ourselves. This challenge often comes in the context of a new church experience. In the context of a job, when supervisors and managers treat us unfairly (either positively or negatively), a response of humility may be difficult.

Deep personal *peace* may have been elusive in college—no contextual change will make that easier to achieve. Yet as disciples of Jesus we are to be people who experience peace. Some people may simply have to reject certain jobs because they cannot perform them and live in peace. Long-term anxiety and faithful seeking of the kingdom of God are incompatible (Matthew 6:25-33).

Priority on people. Unfortunately, in our society jobs that place a priority on people are not as valued as those that deal with technology. So teachers, social workers, pastors and counselors are not as well paid as engineers and doctors. Even in medicine, specialties that are high-tech (low people-intensive) are more highly paid than specialties that are highly relational. Because of the divergence between our society's values and the values of Jesus, followers of his may be on a lower-income track.

The ministry of *hospitality* is perhaps undervalued today. It was a required character trait of those would be chosen as bishops or overseers in the early church (1 Timothy 3:2). In college hospitality involved such simple things as keeping food in your room, baking cookies for people and providing snacks at a Bible study. After college the potential for hospitality (and its cost) rises. You may choose to have a guest room in your house or apartment or an open guest policy for meals in your household.

Mere *availability* puts feet on the desire to be a good friend or servant to someone. Availability makes it happen; good intentions don't. In college you can minister God's grace to someone simply by being available to listen when he or she is going through a difficult time with family, academics or a romantic relationship. This can be costly, because such conversations often begin late at night and can hinder sleep or study. After college a willingness to listen and an ability to listen well are among the rarest of graces in the working world. Again, willingness to listen will be costly, both in time and in emotional energy. But it is part of making people a priority in our lives.

Genuine *forgiveness* is hard to come by in the "real world." The world has no category for asking forgiveness; rather, people tend to excuse themselves or blame others. (Ultimately, the world cannot acknowledge sin because it has no antidote for it.) The fact is that we will sin against non-Christians. And asking them for forgiveness will be even harder: humbling, risky, yet potentially very fruitful, both for our relationships with them and for their understanding of the gospel.

The Lord Is My Shepherd

Our determination to live out the gospel will put us at odds with the world. We will be swimming against the current of society, and this will be exhausting and potentially confusing. Fortunately, Jesus' kingship doesn't simply (or essentially) mean a list of things we need to *do*. Fundamentally it involves entering into a care relationship with the One who really knows our needs and is able to meet them. It means admitting that we cannot take care of ourselves on our own. It means embracing the following picture of the relationship between ourselves and Jesus:

The LORD is my shepherd, I shall not want.
    He makes me lie down in green pastures;
he leads me beside still waters;
    he restores my soul.
He leads me in right paths
    for his name's sake.
Even though I walk through the darkest valley,
    I fear no evil;
for you are with me;
    your rod and your staff—
    they comfort me.
You prepare a table before me
    in the presence of my enemies;
you anoint my head with oil;
    my cup overflows.
Surely goodness and mercy shall follow me
    all the days of my life,
and I shall dwell in the house of the LORD
    my whole life long. (Psalm 23)

The image of God as a shepherd may be lost on those of us who have no everyday knowledge of sheepherding in the ancient Near East.

The shepherd was responsible for seeing that all the needs of the sheep were met. "He makes me lie down" sounds coercive, but in fact sheep won't lie down if they are hungry, thirsty or fearful. Sheep tend to be easily frightened, and even a little movement in the water can be threatening. So the image of a sheep lying down in a green pasture beside still waters is a picture of total contentment.

The psalm is filled with extravagant images of care and protection. The shepherd works hard to guide his sheep; his efforts include effective use of the rod and staff to protect them from predatory animals, to discipline them when they endanger themselves and to pull them out of tight spots they fall into.

Then the psalmist leaves the sheepherding imagery to describe a lush banquet given by the Lord to demonstrate the Lord's favor on him in the presence of his enemies. Needless to say, sitting down at a banqueting table while enemies threaten imminent attack indicates total trust in the Lord's protection. The psalmist's final image is of personified "goodness and mercy," which literally "chase me down" or "pursue me" "all the days of my life." When God is our Lord, goodness and mercy will pursue us. So we see how the thought of the first verse sums up the entire psalm: "The LORD is my shepherd, I lack nothing."

It is not stretching this psalm too much to see it as prophetic of Jesus' leadership. In Ezekiel 34 God promises that he himself will become the shepherd of his people, and in John 10 Jesus claims that he is that "good shepherd" who lays down his life for his sheep so that they may experience abundant life. Having Jesus as our King means that we embrace the care, guidance, discipline and provision of Jesus as our Shepherd.

This image is important for us as we leave college and enter the "real world." Often the phrase "the real world" is used as shorthand for "It's a cold, cruel world out there." Much of our college experience has involved preparing us to be on our own, to stand on our own two feet, alone against the world. Without a Shepherd-King it *is* a "cold, cruel world out there."

In regard to life after college, perhaps the most significant image of the psalm is in the last verse: "Surely goodness and mercy shall follow me all the days of my life." Explicitly or implicitly, we tend to think of our life goals in terms of a pursuit of happiness. In the psalmist's experience, though, the pursuit has been turned around: happiness (goodness and mercy) has pursued *him*, chasing him down even when he, in his blind pursuit of other things, tried to run away.

This has often been my experience of God: he will pursue me for my own good far more readily than I will pursue the things he wants for me. So I receive goodness and mercy at the hand of the Lord, but it is not usually a result of my relentless search; rather, it is a result of the Lord's relentless determination to bless and care for me in spite of my sinful tendency to wander from him.

As you take time to reflect on Psalm 23, you too can identify with the psalmist. Even as our peers are getting ahead of us and everyone seems to be on a faster track than we are, we can rejoice with the psalmist in our relationship with a God who pursues us *for our good*. With that confidence we can continue to make choices to place the control and direction of our lives in his sure and steady hands.

■ *For Reflection*
Leave Your Nets

☐ What is your defining characteristic? If the evangelist were to narrate your encounter with Jesus Christ, what would he mention to describe you?

☐ What "nets" hold you back from following Jesus more fully?

☐ As you continue to respond to Jesus' invitation, what do repentance and belief look like?

"Use the Force, Luke"

☐ How are you tempted to use the instruments of the unbelieving world to give you guidance?

☐ Which of your discipleship convictions do you sense are susceptible to erosion over time?

☐ How can you continue to rely on the power and guidance of Jesus in your life at this time?

Context Changes, Convictions Remain

Spend some time thinking about convictions you have embraced as a disciple of Jesus Christ. Identify which convictions are most central to your life and growth as a Christian. Think first about the application of those convictions in the college setting; then consider how those same convictions could be applied in the new setting you are in or will be in after graduation from college.

The Lord Is My Shepherd

☐ Do you experience God as your Shepherd-King? Can you affirm, with the psalmist, "I lack nothing"?

☐ Do you tend to see yourself pursuing goodness and mercy? How might you need to stop to let God's goodness catch up to you?

☐ How does your life need to change to allow God to be your Shepherd-King?

For Further Reading

Both of the following books help readers examine their assumptions about life and discipleship and offer challenging cultural critiques.

Alexander, John. *The Secular Squeeze*. Downers Grove, Ill.: InterVarsity Press, 1993.

Bascom, Tim. *The Comfort Trap*. Downers Grove, Ill.: InterVarsity Press, 1993.

3
Productivity
and Prayer

A young teenager and an elderly Japanese gardener become friends in the movie *Karate Kid*. Danny has just moved to Los Angeles and is being harassed at his new school. Having learned that Mr. Miyage knows karate, the boy asks to become his pupil. Mr. Miyage agrees and immediately puts Danny to work waxing his many cars and painting his wood fence. Miyage gives him specific instructions regarding his household tasks. "Wax on," he says, moving his right hand in a circle; "wax off," he says, moving his left hand in the opposite circle. Miyage's instructions regarding the manner of waxing and painting are to be obeyed exactly. Danny waxes all the cars and paints the fence but eventually gets impatient. Finally he explodes: "You promised you'd teach me karate. But you just made me your slave!"

At this point Mr. Miyage shows him the relevance of his tasks to his training. "Wax on" and "wax off" were not really techniques to satisfy an uptight slave-driver but exercises designed to build the strength and reflexes necessary for effective karate defense. While the boy was waxing cars and painting fences, he was developing muscles and important foundations for his karate training.

Even after this revelation, Danny is eager to learn how to hit and kick. The master tells him that he must wait, that his fundamental training is defensive and everything else will be built on it.

We are often like the Karate Kid. While God works to train into us fundamental skills for the defense of our discipleship, we want to get on to advanced material, more "productive" things. In our case the "defense" is prayer—taking time to develop our relationship with God. God says to us, "Give yourself to this discipline. It may seem like nonactivity, but it is the foundation of everything of value." Or, as S. D. Gordon once said, "You can do more than pray after you pray, but you cannot do more than pray until you pray."[1] At the beginning of a day, or in the planning of our lives, too often we want to advance quickly without spending quality time with God in prayer.

"You Lack One Thing"

One man who seemed to do well at the advanced material but failed at the basics was the man who approached Jesus in Mark 10.

As he was setting out on a journey, a man ran up and knelt before him, and asked him, "Good Teacher, what must I do to inherit eternal life?" Jesus said to him, "Why do you call me good? No one is good but God alone. You know the commandments: 'You shall not murder; You shall not commit adultery; You shall not steal; You shall not bear false witness; You shall not defraud; Honor your father and mother.' " He said to him, "Teacher, I have kept all these since my youth." Jesus, looking at him, loved him and said, "You lack one thing; go, sell what you own, and give the money to the poor, and you will have treasure in heaven; then come, follow me." When he heard this, he was shocked and went away grieving, for he had many possessions. (vv. 17-22)

On first reading, this incident seems to represent a failure of Jesus' evangelistic strategy. Why did Jesus become picky about the man's choice of words? Why did Jesus answer the man's query about salvation with a works-oriented approach, pointing him to the Ten Commandments instead of faith? Didn't Jesus realize that this guy wasn't ready to give away all his possessions? Almost every sentence Jesus utters in this ninety-second evangelistic encounter seems to be contrary to conventional wisdom regarding how to interest someone in the gospel.

Of course another way to read the story is to conclude that Jesus showed extraordinary insight into this man—and that perhaps the encounter wasn't a failure after all. Jesus knew that the man's trouble began with his concept of himself. He called Jesus "Good Teacher" because of his belief that humans can be good. Jesus responds with a challenge, not to make a claim for his own divinity but to address the issue of the man's sinful humanity. "No one is good but God alone—no human teacher, not even you."

Then Jesus points him to the second table of the law, the last six commandments. The man claims to have obeyed these commandments. Here we might have expected Jesus to denounce the man's pride and call him a liar, but his response is love for the man. Perhaps another way to read this might be, "Jesus, looking at him, loved him [by] saying, 'You lack one thing . . .' " It is out of his love for the young man that Jesus points out his lack.

When Jesus lists some of the Ten Commandments for the man, he leaves out the first four, but not because he has forgotten them. It may seem as if Jesus is listing commandments haphazardly, as if he has a hard time remembering them all, and stopping when he thinks he has mentioned enough to make his point. But Jesus is very intentional here. He leaves out the first four "love God" commands (worship God only, no graven images or idols, don't take God's name in vain, honor the sabbath) because he knows that's where the man's problem lies. The man does fine at loving his neighbor and perhaps is exceptional in this category. His problem is even more fundamental. He does not worship God only; he has another god—his possessions. So when Jesus says, "You lack one thing," the thing the man lacks is love for God. He has never experienced a trust relationship with God.

So why does Jesus tell the man to go, sell, give, come, follow? Why does he tell the man to sell everything? The man's money stands in the way of his ability to see God provide for him. In the imagery from chapter one of this book, the man must let go of his "wealth branch" in order to need and rely on the saving power of Jesus. Or in the closing imagery from chapter two, the man needs to put himself in a position where Jesus can become his Shepherd. In fact, that is exactly what Jesus recommends: "You lack one thing, but if you allow me to be your Shepherd, then you will lack nothing" (see Psalm 23:1).

I think of this man, whom we know from all the Gospels as "the rich young ruler," as a prototype of college graduates today. The man had everything going for him—he was young but accomplished, he had wealth and standing, he had motivation enough to come to Jesus to ask what he should do. I am sure the man half expected Jesus to be impressed enough with his record to tell him he was already doing just fine. To this wealthy young man, and to today's bright young recent graduate, full of potential and educational capital, Jesus says surprising words: "You lack one thing." Other people say, "You have everything going for you," but Jesus disagrees. "No, in fact you lack one thing." One crucial thing.

How to "Serve God" Without Loving God

Often it is easy to discern what other people have as gods and idols in their lives without being able to see our own. Part of what obscures our own idolatry is that we dress it up in spiritual language with well-intentioned goals. For the sake of "serving God" we can forget to honor him or seek him in prayer.

> Now as they went on their way, he entered a certain village, where a woman named Martha welcomed him into her home. She had a sister named Mary, who sat at the Lord's feet and listened to what he was saying. But Martha was distracted by her many tasks; so she came to him and asked, "Lord, do you not care that my sister has left me to do all the work by myself? Tell her then to help me." But the Lord answered her, "Martha, Martha, you are worried and distracted by many things; there is need of only one thing. Mary has chosen the better part, which will not be taken away from her." (Luke 10:38-42)

Jesus has been on the road to Jerusalem since Luke 9:51. That means this is not a private dinner for three, the two sisters and Jesus. Jesus' disciples are with him, at least twelve and possibly more. We can only imagine what kind of stress a crowd of that size would put on Martha and her modest suburban home (located in Bethany, about two miles outside Jerusalem). Martha shoulders the challenge of hospitality for such an honored guest as Jesus but chafes under the strain of it all.

Consider how Martha treats her honored guest. Her question to Jesus stings with sarcasm: "Lord, do you not care?" She knows that Jesus does care, but her question is framed to shame him into action. Then she commands her "Lord" to tell her sister to help her in the kitchen. If Jesus really were her Lord, she should certainly know not to try to issue commands to him. What drives her to this kind of disrespect and harshness?

As I imagine the scene, I suppose Martha's request of Jesus was her last and most desperate attempt to get Mary's attention and convince her to join in the dinner preparation. Consider how the story might have been very different if Mary had been standing outside the circle of the disciples, perhaps at the door of the room. Martha would simply have had to come behind her, gently tap on her shoulder and ask for help. No doubt Mary would have been saddened to leave but would have understood her duty. But in fact Mary was not standing; she was not at the edge of the circle; she was not easily distracted by Martha. Her gaze was fixed on Jesus as she sat as near to him as she could. Martha no doubt motioned to Mary, perhaps whispered to Mary, perhaps moved around the periphery of the room trying to attract Mary's attention, but all to no avail. So she was left with only one very desperate choice, to interrupt the Master in order to seek his help.

But her exasperation at Mary left her with little grace with which to entreat Jesus. She was sarcastic and demanding with the very One whom all of her activity was meant to honor. She was "serving Jesus" without loving him.

As we might expect, however, Jesus is loving and patient with Martha. "Martha, Martha": Jesus utters her name with compassion, not impatience. He *does* care about her; he *has* noticed; he *does* understand her situation. He has seen her efforts on his behalf, but he is aware that they have kept her from listening to him. He doesn't chastise Martha, but he helps her to see that a better option is available to her, the one Mary has chosen.

I am a vision-driven person. I wake up early each morning with my goals for the day clearly in mind. But being involved in student ministry, I often confuse my goals with those of the kingdom of God, and doing my work with seeking the kingdom. Fortunately, there *is* some overlap. But often I am tempted to leave Jesus behind in order to do what I think he wants me to do. Like Martha, I often intend to "serve Jesus" yet fail to love him.

These are issues of productivity *and prayer*. In eternal terms these two are inseparable, but often to us they seem to be contrary. Martha was being so productive there in the kitchen. Should she have just sat down and listened to Jesus too? What would have happened to the dinner? Mary, on the other hand, was focused on Jesus, listening to him. Surely nothing would get done if all we did was imitate her.

The problem is that in our culture, productivity and prayer are not valued equally. They are not simply two equal priorities. Productivity is highly regarded and well remunerated while prayer is neither. So without discipline we will tend to give priority to activities that are highly valued and will barely eke out time to pray.

Years ago Charles Hummel wrote a little book whose title captures the essence of this problem: *Tyranny of the Urgent*.[2] Drawing a distinction between urgent things and important things, Hummel observed that too often our lives are ruled by the apparent need to get urgent things done, while the important things, because they are not urgent, remain undone. This is true about many activities, but especially prayer. Though we all know prayer is extremely important, something is always ready to crowd our time or to capture our attention so that we cannot pray.

Choose the Better Part

We have looked at the story in Luke 10 from Martha's perspective, understanding both her drive to serve Jesus and the frustration with Mary's apparent lack of concern. Consider the same story from Mary's perspective.

Mary too was excited about the chance to have Jesus honor her family's house by sharing a meal with them. When Jesus came and

sat down to teach, Mary watched as the disciples filled out the circle
in the gathering room. Spying a spot right next to Jesus' feet, she
eventually took it as hers for the afternoon. So intent on hearing from
Jesus, so grateful for his every word was Mary that she didn't even see
or hear her sister's repeated attempts to get her attention. From where
she sat, she simply couldn't be distracted by Martha's antics. She remained focused on what was really important that afternoon in Bethany. Therefore Jesus says in her defense, "Mary has chosen the better
part, which will not be taken away from her."

Mary is an excellent model for the recent or soon-to-be graduate.
During this time of transition many distractions fill our minds, our
appointment books, our "to do" lists. Applications, résumés, interviews, financial aid forms, the impending repayment of student loans,
the search for housing and housemates, the uncertainty of changing
relationships—all these things can provide fodder for a Martha-like
expostulation: "Jesus, don't you care that I am about to graduate?"

Yet Mary's desire was to be next to Jesus, close to him, listening
intently to him. Proximity to Jesus actually kept Mary safe from the
tyranny of the urgent, from the intrusion of the demands of the day
on her sense of priorities.

I say that Mary's proximity kept her *safe* because, in fact, she was
endangered by Martha. Mary had made a choice to listen to Jesus, but
we know that such a choice is always open to renegotiation. When we
choose to follow Jesus, to be directed by him, that is not a once-for-
all-time decision. So the closer we place ourselves to Jesus, the more
fully he has our attention, the safer we are. When we allow ourselves
to take a comfortable seat in the back row, listening to Jesus but
allowing our eyes and minds to wander, we open ourselves up to the
danger of the distractions of the day. Even a misplaced desire to be
productive for the kingdom of God can keep us from submission to
the good and perfect will of the King.

What Jesus says to Martha he could easily say to any of us: "Student,
student [or Graduate, graduate], you are worried and distracted by
many things; there is need of only one thing." While our non-Christian peers are all too eager to enter the rat race, we can be safe-

guarded from its exacting demands by listening to Jesus. If we take time to sit at his feet, listening to him rather than simply listing our requests, we may find that Jesus doesn't want us to race like rats. We may come to hear his higher call on our lives.

■ For Reflection
"You Lack One Thing"
☐ If Jesus were to say to you in love, "You lack one thing," what lack would he point to in your life?

☐ What keeps you from experiencing the Shepherd-King love of Jesus? From placing your trust fully in him?

How to "Serve God" Without Loving God
☐ As you think about all the choices you face, are your prayer times eroded by distraction? How do you experience the "tyranny of the urgent"?

Choose the Better Part
In the morning I am often distracted by the upcoming events or concerns of the day. Instead of bringing these to Jesus for his care, I usually stop praying and start focusing on my concerns. Sometimes this catapults me out of prayer and into my day's activity without so much as a second thought. Sometimes, however, I am able to refocus, turn the distractions over to Jesus and allow him to protect me from the claims of my would-be tyrants.

☐ What are you distracted by in the morning when your desire is to turn your thoughts to the Lord?

☐ What does it mean for you to sit near Jesus, at his feet, rather than to stand at a distance?

Please, before you read on or turn to do other things, take some time now to pray.

For Further Reading
Hybels, Bill. *Too Busy Not to Pray.* Downers Grove, Ill.: InterVarsity Press, 1988.

4
Meaningless Work and Fruitful Labor

Melinda graduated and went to work in a consulting firm in Boston. She had been a leader in her college Christian fellowship and was eager to continue to grow in her discipleship after college. But she soon found that the work demanded of her took most of her waking hours each week. She had taken the job partly because she was told that she would be working fifty-five hours a week, on average. Though this was high, she thought she could handle it and still pursue her faith through church involvement, a young-adults Bible study and relationships with Christian friends in the Boston area.

After six months of work averaging over sixty-five hours a week, Melinda decided that she needed to do more than make subtle suggestions to her supervisor, a senior partner in her firm, that she was being overworked. Her job involved making presentations to clients with proposals for new or revised business strategies and management plans. She decided to make a similar presentation to her boss, discussing her own priorities and the conflict between work demands and her desire to pursue other goals. She was very clear with her supervisor that making money or succeeding in her career was not her goal in working for the firm. Her goals included learning business, organization and presentation skills but also developing spiritually and maintaining deep friendships. She documented how it was impossible to satisfy her goals on a sixty-five-hours-a-week schedule. Making it clear that the current situation was not tenable long-term, she suggested various ways that her work schedule could be reduced. She said she was even prepared to accept a lower salary in return for a lighter workload. Though she was a valued worker, she knew that this presentation could result in her being fired. As with Nehemiah making his petition before King Artaxerxes (Nehemiah 2:1), Melinda's fate lay in the hands of the authority figure she challenged.

She was not fired. Melinda's supervisor was impressed with the work she had done to communicate her dissatisfaction in terms he could readily understand. Her workload *was* reduced—not without cost to Melinda, for her year-end bonus was substantially reduced from the previous year and her performance reviews were more critical. Within a few months, however, her supervisor asked if she would join the nonprofit health-care firm he had started. Though this new job paid less, it was more satisfying and less stressful. The benefits Melinda received far outweighed the costs: she had found a way to pursue committed discipleship after college.

Working for a Living?

Of all the variables in our lives, one virtual certainty is that we will all have a job, at least for some time. But let me ask, Why get a job? If you are working now, why? If you are looking for a job, why? This is not a trick question.

The most common reason to work is to make money, to provide for necessities. Even the familiar question implies this: "What do you do for a living?" The question assumes that the activity you do that pays a salary or wage is the activity you do in order to live.

Of course we can recognize many other good reasons to work: to pay back student loans, to help out one's family, for enjoyment, for

a challenge, to make a meaningful contribution to society, for fulfillment, to be able to give to others in need. But these all seem second-
ary in some way. If you found a job that provided all of these but left
you with no money for food or clothing or rent, you probably would
be forced to look for a new job. On the other hand, many people find
almost none of these other satisfactions in their jobs. They have
settled for simply working for a living.[1]

When work becomes simply a means for survival, we have traded
away much of the value and purposefulness that God intended for
work. We begin to think that we are working only so that one day—
the weekend, a vacation or retirement—we won't have to! When we
think of work, the only thing we thank God for is the fact that it is
Friday—TGIF!

Let's not settle for simply working for a living. We need to reject our
culture's attitudes toward work and embrace a biblical view.

Facing the prospect of leaving the security of the college environment, you may be tempted to take the first job that offers a decent
wage. Yet Jesus calls those who want to be his disciples not to settle
for this petty vision.

Striving for the Kingdom

A complete biblical picture of work is beyond the scope of this book.
Entire books have been written to address the topic. So let me just
summarize some fundamental biblical truths regarding work.

☐ God *created, formed, shaped, fixed, handled* creation; that is, God was
the first worker (Genesis 1). Jesus, as God incarnate, spent most of his
adult life working as a carpenter. The dignity of human work is revealed in this: God came to earth and made furniture.

☐ Humanity is created in the image of God the Worker and was given
work to do *before* the Fall (Genesis 1:28; 2:15). Human work reflects
the image of God. While still in the Garden of Eden, Adam had work
to do.

☐ As a result of Adam and Eve's sin, God cursed the ground and work
became *toil* (Genesis 3:17-19). Since the Fall all work is fundamentally
thwarted—it doesn't go as planned, involves sweat and effort, and

ultimately humans and their labors return to dust. Yet work itself is not a result of the curse.

These observations from Genesis provide a foundation from which to examine the relationship of work and the kingdom of God.

Therefore I tell you, do not worry about your life, what you will eat or what you will drink, or about your body, what you will wear. Is not life more than food, and the body more than clothing? Look at the birds of the air; they neither sow nor reap nor gather into barns, and yet your heavenly Father feeds them. Are you not of more value than they? And can any of you by worrying add a single hour to your span of life? And why do you worry about clothing? Consider the lilies of the field, how they grow; they neither toil nor spin, yet I tell you, even Solomon in all his glory was not clothed like one of these. But if God so clothes the grass of the field, which is alive today and tomorrow is thrown into the oven, will he not much more clothe you—you of little faith? Therefore do not worry, saying, "What will we eat?" or "What will we drink?" or "What will we wear?" For it is the Gentiles who strive for all these things; and indeed your heavenly Father knows that you need all these things. But strive first for the kingdom of God and his righteousness, and all these things will be given to you as well.

So do not worry about tomorrow, for tomorrow will bring worries of its own. Today's trouble is enough for today. (Matthew 6:25-34)

The Sermon on the Mount is the most impractical practical teaching Jesus ever delivered. Here Jesus describes the culture of the kingdom of God. He challenges his disciples to embrace a countercultural reality, identity and loyalty. In this section Jesus addresses a very natural tendency to worry about the essentials of life—food, drink, clothing—but he tells his disciples, "Don't worry; instead strive for the kingdom."

Note that Jesus doesn't say, "Don't worry, don't strive." Something *is* worth striving for. Scripture repeatedly warns against laziness and idleness (for example, Proverbs 6:6-11), and Paul warns believers to stay away from able-bodied people who have made a conscious choice not to work; these people, he says, should not be supported (2 Thessalonians 3:6-10). They, along with many in our society, should be called to repent of their attitude, for they have lost sight of God's good purpose in work and have idolized leisure.

Notice also that Jesus doesn't say, "Strive first for the kingdom; then you'll have plenty of time to strive for food, clothes and other things." He is not suggesting that having a "quiet time" at the beginning of the day frees us to spend the rest of the day striving for our necessities. In fact, he specifically warns *against* striving for these things.

The question then, of course, is, How will we eat? Jesus has that most impractical practical answer: God will provide for us.

Jesus divides our pursuits into two categories, those that are our responsibility and those that are God's. *Our* responsibility is to strive for the kingdom of God. Our energy, time and attention are to be focused there. This will include working a job, but as an act of faithfulness to God, not as an anxiety-producing economic pursuit. *God's* work is to provide for us: food, clothing, shelter, all the worrisome needs we have. And he promises to do so, if we are striving first for his kingdom.

The economy of our culture is a closed system. It assumes a one-to-one relationship between the financial rewards of work and physical needs: you work to live, to support yourself. (This is not to fail to recognize the other rewards of work.) According to Jesus, however, the system is not closed: God makes all of his resources available to us as we strive for the kingdom. We don't have to look out for our own needs, because the God of the universe is responsible for that task and he is more than able to handle it.

Here Jesus is not making a promise that hasn't ever been made before in salvation history. From Eden to the Sinai desert to the land of Canaan to the exile, God's promise to his people has always been, "If you let me guide you, you will not be in need." The sheep's responsibility is simply to follow the Shepherd. The Shepherd-Lord's responsibility is to provide food, comfort, rest, cool water and protection (Psalm 23).

This means we don't have to fear the consequences of pursuing discipleship. This can be tremendously freeing. Losing one's job in order to remain faithful to Jesus need not be threatening. If by striving for the kingdom we cannot carry out our jobs, either because of a conflict of conscience or because of a conflict of purpose, we can be assured that God will provide for us in another way. It may mean a severe cut in income, and that might be a shock to our system. We may even experience suffering and privation, but we have the assurance of God's presence and mercy in the midst of it. My own experience of this, and that of many I know who have made choices to live this way, is that God *does* provide as he has promised.

Of course, throughout Scripture the promises of provision are always made in the context of the people of God, the community of the kingdom, the corporate body of followers who band together to rely on God and the resources he has put in their midst. If we are going to take Jesus seriously here (and I hope we do!), we will need to join with others who are doing that as well. (This I will take up in more detail in the next two chapters.)

God is the one who takes responsibility for providing for us, *not our employer.* God may be currently using the company we work for to provide us with salary enough to satisfy our daily needs, but that could change at any time without any lessening of God's faithfulness or his ability to provide.

So when Melinda faced her supervisor with her request for a decreased workload, she could do so without paralyzing fear that she would be fired. Certainly Melinda *hoped* she wouldn't be fired. But she could trust that God was leading her and would provide for her, whether through her current job or through another. Her responsibility was to strive for the kingdom. And God proved faithful to her as she placed her trust in him.

Fruitful Labor

Paul's letter to the Philippians is a ministry report to his supporters. Things look dim: Paul is in prison, aware that he may be put to death. Yet he writes because he wants the Philippians to know that his imprisonment hasn't been such a terrible thing. In fact, the gospel has been advanced because of it.

For to me, living is Christ and dying is gain. If I am to live in the

flesh, that means fruitful labor for me; and I do not know which
I prefer. I am hard pressed between the two: my desire is to depart
and be with Christ, for that is far better; but to remain in the flesh
is more necessary for you. (Philippians 1:21-24)

Paul speaks of his two choices: life or death, Christ or gain. He is
attracted to dying, because that means he would go and be with Christ.
But he determines that he will remain alive in order to help people
like the Philippians continue to grow as disciples of Jesus.

There is a strange logic at work in this passage. Paul decides that
he will "choose" to stay alive—as any of us might do—but for very
different reasons from those that would motivate most of us. Paul's
perspective is so clear that he not only doesn't fear death but would
gladly welcome release from this life into the bliss to come. So it is
not survival instinct that keeps Paul alive. What then? The chance to
pursue fruitful labor.

Paul has reversed the normal relationship between working and
living. The common conception is that we work "for a living"—we
work to live. Instead Paul lives to work, to pursue "fruitful labor,"
which in this context can only mean fruitful in the spiritual sense.
Paul lives in order to be in ministry to the people of God, to help them
grow in their faith. Not only is Paul not striving for food and clothing
in order to live, but he remains alive simply to strive for the kingdom.
Paul stays alive in order to advance the kingdom, to lose his life for
Jesus' sake and to find real life.

I suppose we could say, "That was Paul. I am not called to live like
Paul did." Yet Jesus told us to have the same attitude Paul did toward
fruitful labor: "Do not work for the food that perishes, but for the food
that endures for eternal life, which the Son of Man will give you. For
it is on him that God the Father has set his seal" (John 6:27).

Jesus doesn't want any of his followers to waste their time laboring
for food that rots tomorrow or is eaten and then no longer satisfies.
Jesus wants all of us to labor for that which produces eternal fruit,
eternal life for ourselves and for others. And the night before he was
crucified he gave his disciples a vision of their life after his ascension:
"You did not choose me but I chose you. And I appointed you to go

and bear fruit, *fruit that will last"* (John 15:16).

Each of us has a deep need to know that what we do with our labor will mean something, will be significant, will have lasting consequences. Jesus knows our need. He promises us that he has the same intention. Jesus says to each of us, "I have chosen you to live a life that has lasting, eternal consequences. Don't spend your life for things that do not last; do not labor for that which does not satisfy" (see Isaiah 55:2).

This is not to say that non-Christians cannot work jobs that give some measure of fulfillment, or that the only fulfilling jobs involve "full-time Christian ministry." Remember, work was given to humans before the Fall (Genesis 2:15), and all legitimate work is valuable and able to bring some fulfillment. But with the Fall, work became difficult and the results of our labor temporary (Genesis 3:17-19). Hence no work is ever totally fulfilling. And apart from the advance of the kingdom of God, none of our efforts are guaranteed to have lasting effect.

So Jesus redeems us from the effects of the Fall and its curse. He does this not by redeeming us from striving but by making our striving purposeful, yielding lasting fruit.

The Relationship Between Work and Needs

We are to strive for the kingdom of God rather than for our daily necessities. Is there then any correlation between work and daily needs? Look at Ephesians 4:28: "Thieves must give up stealing; rather let them labor and work honestly with their own hands . . ."

This is Paul's advice to thieves who up to this point have not worked with their hands, except dishonestly. He tells them to give up stealing and begin working. But what is the reason he gives? How would you expect Paul to finish his sentence?

"Let them work honestly with their own hands so that they won't have to steal anymore."

"Let them do honest work to feed themselves."

"Let them do honest work so that they are not leeches on society."

Paul doesn't say any of these things. Instead Paul calls the former thieves into ministry: "[Let them do honest work] so as to have something to share with the needy." The purpose of the honest work of the former thieves is to transform it into *fruitful labor.* They aren't just working to support themselves. No one in the economy of God works merely to support himself or herself. Paul is saying, "Part of the reason God has you in that job is to take care of the needs of others." God may be taking care of the needs of others, as he has promised them, through the resources he has entrusted to you through your job.

What then is the relationship between our work and needs? We work to be able to provide for the needs of others; we are all called into ministry in this way. All of us are supposed to strive first for the kingdom of God, trusting God to provide for us, using the resources entrusted to us to provide for others.

Vocation and Tents

When Christians talk about work, jobs and careers they often use the word *vocation.* This is an ancient word, coming from the Latin *vocare,* "to call." Literally vocation is a calling, and for Christians it is understood as a "calling from God." Yet the reality is that Jesus' clearest call on our lives is the call he issued to his first and all subsequent disciples: "Follow me and I will make you fishers of people," and "Strive first for the kingdom of God." In all of Scripture the term *calling* is never directly associated with a job or profession.[2]

Of course this definition does not solve the problem of what to do with our time, but it at least clarifies the priority. Jesus' call is to make our first priority striving for the kingdom, losing our life for his sake and the gospel's, working for food that endures to eternal life, bearing lasting fruit. So if our vocation (striving for the kingdom) isn't up in the air, what remains is a question not of *vocation* but of *location.*

How often have you prayed, "God, please show me your will for my life"? Really we should ask a different question: What does God value? John Perkins claims, "God's will is plain. We are to love him and to love people."[3] God's will for my life has much more to do with my embracing his plan and desire for the world than with my finding God's particular plan for my success and comfort. We are to use the work we do to love God and to love others.

Scripture speaks with great clarity. We don't need to pray, "Let me know your will so I can follow you." He has already revealed his will. The remaining question is, How can I find my life in God's will?[4] We must turn the common, secular or even Christian misconception of vocation upside down: God has a will, and he has made it very plain. He calls us to join what he is doing and to value what he values. In this we find life.

This is not to say that there is only one way to strive for the kingdom or live in the will of God. There are many legitimate ways to allocate one's time so as to reflect the priorities of God and of God's kingdom.

In Scripture we find many models of work and ministry. For example, we learn in Acts 18:3 that Paul was by trade a tentmaker. He worked at his trade in order to provide for himself and his traveling companions as he preached the gospel from town to town (Acts 20:34; 1 Thessalonians 2:9). In 1 Corinthians 9 Paul gives us insight into why he lived this way. Though as an apostle he could be entitled to live on support, he says, "We have not made use of this right, but we endure anything rather than put an obstacle in the way of the gospel of Christ" (1 Corinthians 9:12). In other words, Paul is a tentmaker for the sake of the kingdom. His "fruitful labor" is not making tents but seeking and advancing the kingdom; he makes tents in order to advance his overall (and single) goal.

Paul's life was not dichotomized into his ministry life and his work life. Paul understood his whole life as striving for the kingdom, whether through making tents or through preaching. But it also meant that when he was thrown into prison he didn't view that as a blow to his tentmaking business, but actually as a boon to his evangelistic ministry. In jail Paul could witness to guards and write letters to his partner churches.

Though Paul understood his tentmaking as a support to his ministry (and not *as* his ministry), there is a sense that his tentmaking also provided a useful product. Unlike most tents sold in Western nations today, Paul's tents provided fundamental, not simply recreational, housing for his customers. Shelter is a fundamental need, and addressing that need is a valuable enterprise. While Paul didn't glorify his tentmaking activity as his ministry, we can assume that he worked with diligence and honesty to make quality tents that would last.

Like Paul, we want to be people who can say at the end of a week, "I have been fully involved in striving for the kingdom. All of my resources, my time and energy, have been mobilized toward the kingdom." Not just two hours on Thursday nights or three hours on Sunday mornings—we want to live our whole lives in a way that will make a difference eternally, so we bear fruit that will last. Jesus has called us to this.

Models of Work and Ministry

Most jobs could lend themselves to striving for the kingdom, but not every job automatically does. Often our assumptions and attitudes will determine whether we are striving for the kingdom or simply making a living, finding life or ultimately losing our lives.

There are many legitimate models for the allocation of one's time. Some people work as "tentmakers" while their focus of ministry is in another area. Some work as ministers of the gospel and are supported fully by that ministry. Some work part time to free much time for ministry outside of work. Others work full time in jobs that are a key part of their ministry. Let's consider a few specific examples as models of work and ministry. (I will discuss more about ministry and give a definition of it in chapter eight.)

1. Full-time secular employment: Accountant

Ministry opportunities. It is possible to invest your time and energy in kingdom-directed activity in a number of ways on the job:

☐ Listening to and caring for coworkers. As discussed in chapter two, listening to people can be a powerful ministry, rare but vitally needed in the workplace. You can offer friendship and counsel with gospel content.

☐ Displaying personal integrity and moral character through honesty in expense accounts, being above reproach in relationships with people of the opposite sex, accepting blame and sharing credit rather than vice versa. A life of integrity—a consistency between beliefs and actions—can be a powerful witness to others.

☐ Speaking up. Silent witness is not the only witness. Be ready to speak up regarding the truth you know and the hope that you have (1 Peter 3:15), though often people may subtly dismiss you when you do this. Your integrity will make all the difference in how people receive your words.

☐ Conducting your work ethically: pursuing integrity in accounting standards, giving an honest statement of the value of your services.

☐ Earning sufficient funds to provide for others. (See below.)

Other opportunities to find kingdom value and satisfaction in your work:

☐ Provide a product that has socially redeeming value. Does your company's product fill a real need, not simply a need concocted by Madison Avenue advertising executives? This can be a key criterion in choosing work and an employer.

☐ You may be able to shape certain practices of the company by the values of the kingdom of God. Obvious first steps would involve refusing to use your accounting skill to evade taxes or to overstate (or understate) the financial strength of the company, division or department for which you work. More significant might be to encourage and help the company to use a part of its profits or depreciating assets to benefit needy people.

☐ Ministry opportunities beyond the work setting include any number of volunteer activities, whether through church or in other contexts. If you work in accounting or a related field, you would do well to look for a ministry setting where you can get to know a few people well, since the job setting itself doesn't foster deep relationships. Also, if you have a job like this you really should hope to be providing for more than your own needs. Generosity and hospitality are critical as you strive for the kingdom. Look for ways to be diverting the financial resources God has entrusted to you (that is, your salary) to substantially provide for the needs of others. (For more discussion of generosity and hospitality, see chapter seven.)

Dangers. This kind of work probably involves the closest engagement with the world and therefore the greatest temptation to swallow the values of the world. All work settings are risky without partnership, but perhaps this is the riskiest. You will need others who can hold you accountable to your goals and who can sense danger if you are beginning to capitulate to the work culture. Danger signals would include increased work hours, inability to focus on anything but work, inability to make and keep nonwork commitments like church ministry, community service, small group meetings or meals with friends. It is the clear sense of striving for the kingdom that lets you manage work rather than letting it manage you. Expect some conflict at work, and be nervous if you don't sense it. Because so many employees are willing to order their lives around the company, those who refuse will experience tension.

Every company and government agency has its own "corporate culture," a set of values that guide a variety of nonformalized operations from simple social interactions to complex decision-making processes. It is crucial to evaluate the corporate culture of a firm, company or agency against the values of the kingdom. No corporate enterprise will fully affirm God's values, but some companies will do better than others. As you consider where to work, reject a company whose corporate culture is inhospitable to the values of the kingdom. And once you settle on a job, don't confuse your firm's corporate culture with that of the kingdom.

These kinds of jobs are often compensated very well, and one obvious danger is the tendency of one's lifestyle to float up to match one's income. This is a danger because it could erode the very tentmaking purpose that should motivate a Christian's choice of a job like this. Chapter five addresses the critical topic of community, essential to battling this universal tendency.

Other examples: manufacturing business (sales, marketing, product engineering, finance), law, banking, administration, journalism, management, engineering, real estate, medical specialties, academic research.

2. Full-time secular employment: Schoolteacher

Ministry opportunities. Though explicit in-class witness is forbidden for public school teachers, teaching can still provide excellent opportunities for ministry. With the breakdown of the family and the resulting loss of discipline, the ministry of teaching has become much more difficult. As teachers have to fear more for their safety, simply treating students as valuable human beings and not as dangerous threats can be tremendously healing for kids. More than ever before, this ministry is a ministry of fundamentals: bringing love into loveless lives, bringing hope into seemingly hopeless contexts.

A teacher has many avenues into the hearts of children for kingdom influence. Teachers can promote character development through value codes, emphasizing respect for others, cooperation (not simply competition), a sense of belonging to a community and service to others. Through classroom rules, group activities and focusing on role models, even public school teachers can teach gospel values without teaching Christianity. Furthermore, beyond the classroom teachers can give explicit witness to their faith through extracurricular involvement in the lives of kids. (See the story of Jennifer at the beginning of chapter eight for a good example of this.)

Teaching can be a very strategic ministry, whether over the course of a single year or over the course of a career. In most kids' lives you will make a little difference, in a few kids' lives a big difference; over time even small changes can have enormous impact. Because these changes are difficult to measure, you must have a confidence that God is at work and a deep sense of purpose to sustain you when you have little evidence of immediate success.

Dangers. For teachers, the potential for burnout is high. Teaching is not simply a job but an investment of energy and care in a group of relatively needy people. As in many such jobs, maintaining a sense of priority and balance can be difficult. We can forget that ultimately people need God, not us. Jesus alone can save. Specific challenges include the following:

☐ Teaching can swallow your whole life, taking away from your time for church or ministry involvement and other relationships.

☐ Teachers can easily lose sight of what is *important* in the face of all that is *urgent:* preparing and grading tests, assignments and papers.

(See chapter three's discussion of the "tyranny of the urgent.")

☐ It is easy to overlook the needs of the entire class because of the seemingly infinite demands of the neediest of the kids.

☐ It may be difficult to feel partnership in or support for your efforts to minister while teaching. Teaching often consumes many hours beyond forty per week. When you have a kingdom purpose in mind, this can be satisfying, but if your purpose is lost or difficult to sustain, the energy required can be draining. Look for a partner at school or another teacher in your church with whom you can pray for your crucial ministry.

Other examples: social work, primary-care medicine and nursing, public service law, counseling, job placement, child care, teaching English as a second language.

3. Part-time tentmaker: Print Shop Worker

Ministry opportunities. On the job you have many of the same ministry opportunities as Christians in the business world do: listening, consideration, willing servanthood to both customers and coworkers. Occasionally you may be able to share explicitly about your faith, but that will probably be rare.

The real strength of this kind of work situation is the potential for ministry outside the work setting. Because the job is only part-time, large blocks of time and energy are available for intentional ministry, perhaps as a volunteer with a church or parachurch ministry. Because of the nature of the work you do, your mental and creative energy are more fully available for your unpaid ministry involvement. Also, unlike teachers, social workers and counselors, you can leave work for your ministry setting without feeling that your relational energy has been spent. You are able to engage with people in a fresh way.

A part-time tentmaker is doing well if he or she is able simply to provide for living expenses while working part-time. But no matter how little you make, plan to honor God with at least a tithe—10 percent.

I consider this work situation one of the best for recent college graduates. (I myself worked part time for two years after I graduated.)

While there are dangers, mainly I think of this option as a powerful way to avoid many of the dangers of long-term jobs while you are clarifying a sense of call.

Dangers. One of the dangers, surprisingly enough, is the likelihood of experiencing some success in both your work and your unpaid ministry settings. You may experience success and find meaningful ministry in your work setting. Your employer may respond by asking you to work even more hours or simply giving you more work than you can do in your original part-time work schedule. At the same time you may experience real enjoyment and satisfaction in your nonwork ministry setting. You may be asked to give more time to this involvement as well.

While success in both areas seems like a happy problem to have to deal with, success is a difficult thing to turn away from. Sometimes in order to continue striving for the kingdom you may need to make a difficult choice. You may need to quit a job you enjoyed, excelled at and were affirmed for in order to be more available for the fruitful labor God has called you to. On the other hand, if the fruitful labor you are experiencing is primarily in your workplace, you may need to consider refocusing your ministry and allocating more time to your job.

A second danger in part-time work is the potential for laziness. Working part time is not to be an excuse for a lazy, undisciplined life. Many volunteer ministry settings are relatively unstructured. If you do not have self-discipline and self-motivation, this option is not for you.

Other examples: retail sales, office/clerical work, waiting tables, making deliveries, substitute teaching.

4. Full-time Christian ministry: Youth Ministry Worker

Ministry opportunities. The best thing about this option is that you have your full time available for ministry. The breadth of ministry options is so wide I won't even try to do it justice. For persons in this setting, the way God provides the daily necessities that he has promised to cover is through the gifts of people who are involved in the previous three work contexts.

Dangers. Despite the advantages, there are many dangers to this kind of work situation. One is falling into spiritual complacency because you receive a paycheck from a Christian organization or church. Any of us can think of far too many recent examples of ministry leaders who have fallen into sin—illicit sex, deception, pride, greed. Being in professional ministry doesn't make you holy or immune to temptation. On the contrary, it makes you more of a target for Satan's ploys, because the stakes are higher; a fall can affect many people.

As with option 3, this type of work is completely inappropriate for people who are not self-disciplined. The potential fluidity of lifestyle and lack of structure in a ministry environment make this job more difficult than you might imagine.

On the other hand, for highly motivated and disciplined people a more likely danger is experiencing burnout without deep and meaningful partnerships. The nature of most paid Christian ministry is that the work is never done. At the end of a day or week you could always have done more. For people who are moved by the needs of others, this can produce stress and anxiety. Without partners and people to whom you can be accountable for choices about how to spend time, you can easily burn out.

One final danger is the potential to teach irresponsibly. James 3:1 warns that teachers must be careful what they teach and how they live because they will be judged more strictly. Consider carefully whether it is God's call for you to enter into a ministry position where you will have spiritual authority in the lives of others.

Other examples: missionary, pastor.

5. Full-time ministry: Non-Wage-Earning Parent

Ministry opportunities. Clearly, raising children is a ministry and can be a part of striving for the kingdom. Parenthood demands servanthood, the ability to look to the needs of others before your own. Full-time parenthood can be a ministry with great potential for kingdom impact—immediately in the life of your children and indirectly in the lives of all those affected in years to come through growing and grown children who themselves pursue the kingdom of God.

Also, full-time parenthood offers many opportunities for ministry to others beyond the family. Parents can participate in their community through school involvement, including addressing issues of school curriculum, artistic or recreational opportunities (coaching a team sport, for example) or social service.

Dangers. It is possible to equate an almost idolatrous devotion to kids and family with pursuit of the kingdom. Parents can confuse ministry to kids with merely buying things for them, or a focus on the kingdom with a "focus on the family." What begins as a desire to receive children and welcome them in Jesus' name can replace Jesus as the focus of our lives.

It is also possible for the non-wage-earning parent to experience a form of ministry burnout, especially without much partnership or recognition of the value of the choice not to earn a wage. Sometimes because of traditional expectations about gender roles or modern assumptions regarding fulfillment in careers, the choice of full-time motherhood is especially undervalued.

Praying for and Finding a Job

> You do not have, because you do not ask. You ask and do not receive, because you ask wrongly, in order to spend what you get on your pleasures. . . . Do you not know that friendship with the world is enmity with God? (James 4:2-4)

Scripture gives us many promises that God hears and answers prayer. But here we have a warning: motives are critical. *Why we pray* matters. Probably most of us have prayed for a job. But what motivates us to pray for that job is critical.

Why do you pray for a job? Since the above discussion has decoupled work and providing for daily needs, let's identify faithful motives for desiring a job and asking God to lead us to the right one.

☐ *Work as a means of loving and trusting God.* When we are doing what God created us to do, we receive God's blessing in joy and contentment. When we give of our "first fruits"—that is, a tithe off the top—we remind ourselves that all we have comes from him.

☐ *Work as a means of character development.* Many aspects of discipleship are best addressed in the work setting: integrity, submission to
authority, discipline. We are created to become workers.

☐ *Work as a means of loving others.* Work offers a setting in which to
encounter people in need of the gospel. It also supplies us with resources to provide for people in need and to support others in ministry.

When we pray for a job, we also often pray for God's guidance.
Perhaps he will bless us with a choice between jobs, or an unexpected
opportunity. How do we discern God's leading?

A more specific sense of God's guidance may occur through seemingly unconnected events that weave together to form a pattern in the
tapestry of our lives. After graduation Amy eventually found a job as
an administrative assistant for a nonprofit medical-research foundation. She viewed her job mainly as a support to her ministry in and
through her church; her job was second priority in her life. Yet Amy
was a good listener and made friends quickly with others in the office.
She was soon recognized for her competence and asked to apply for
a job as development coordinator.

When Amy was offered the position, it became clear that her time
would be somewhat less available for her ministry commitments. She
would have occasional travel and social responsibilities if she were to
take this new position. What should Amy do? How was God leading?

Amy took the job, but she did not do so because it offered her
substantially more money and more status (which it did). God had
already provided for her physical needs. Rather, she took the job
because of the potential for training and growth. The development
skills she would acquire in her new role would be usable in the future.
As she grew in self-understanding, she could see that this was an area
of interest and God-giftedness for her.

Furthermore, she used her larger paycheck to generously support
her church and worked hard to maintain partnerships there. She was
able to hire another member of her church to take her former position, giving her partnership on the job. Her relationships with the
office staff continued to grow, reflecting her value of people and

disregarding the accepted barriers between hourly and salaried workers in that office. God used this sequence of events in Amy's life to direct her into an area of giftedness and kingdom usefulness. God was preparing Amy for a life of fruitful labor.

Finally, when we find a job we are to be grateful to God for his gift to us. We could easily forget this and slide into one of two sinful attitudes toward our work: resentment and jealousy, or pride.

Jesus tells a story (Matthew 20:1-15) about a landowner who hired laborers for his field. Some workers worked only one hour while some worked twelve, but he paid them all the same. The all-day workers resented the fact that some worked only one hour but received equal pay. To their complaints the landowner replied, "Friend, I am doing you no wrong; did you not agree with me for the usual daily wage? Take what belongs to you and go; I choose to give to this last the same as I give to you. Am I not allowed to do what I choose with what belongs to me? Or are you envious because I am generous?" (vv. 13-15).

Jesus' story challenges us not to resent God's generosity to others. One way we might be tempted is to compare wages and jobs. We could easily come to resent even God's good gift of a job and to be jealous of his gifts to others. We are called to be content with what we have, honoring God as a generous God.

On the other hand, if God does give us a job with great material rewards, it is easy to forget that these are God's resources, meant to be used to honor him and to serve the needs of others. We can take a false pride in our wealth, thinking of it the way the rich fool did: "Soul, you have ample goods laid up for many years; relax, eat, drink, and be merry" (Luke 12:19). Jesus warns us of the foolishness of this attitude as well.

God's Values and the World's Values

As subjects of the King of the kingdom of God, we will often work at cross-purposes to the values of the world's culture. We will challenge the world's assumptions. In one sense, work in the world is valuable to the extent that we, through the way we live and work, undermine

Godless culture and positively live out the values of the kingdom.

Whether you work for a high-tech firm or teach kindergarten, you will experience conflicts in work settings, because the kingdom of God is radically different from the culture we live and work in. When these conflicts come, it is crucial to remember that it is God, not your employ-

	The values of the world	The values of the kingdom
View of the pursuit of work	"The rat race"	Pursuing a sense of *calling*
Who is honored	Those who have escaped "the rat race"; those who live in leisure	We worship a worker God and a worker Savior, Jesus
Purpose of work	People work for a living	We strive for the kingdom; God provides for our necessities
Vision of paradise	The end of "the rat race": paradise involves only play and leisure	The biblical vision of Eden includes purposeful work
View of greatness	Climbing the ladder, entering the professions, being well paid	"Downward mobility," servanthood, becoming last of all
View of redemption	Winning the lottery or making it big eliminates the need to work	Jesus' redemption transforms "toil" into fruitful and lasting labor
View of security	Financial security: we always need a little more money	We bank our hope for a happy future on the promises of God
Source of satisfaction	Achievement and self-reliance	Fulfilling our calling and reliance on God
View of resources and earnings	Ownership: the purpose of money is to satisfy our own needs and desires, and those of our immediate families	Stewardship: resources are entrusted to us, in part, to satisfy the needs of others, especially those in greatest need

er, who provides for you in daily ways. You can face the possibility that the job may end yet find yourself free of anxiety regarding God's ability to provide for you. Melinda faced this prospect and remained faithful. It was her willingness even to lose her job that ultimately led to God's provision of a better work situation.

Yet the divergence between the values of the world and the values of the kingdom presents real danger to disciples of Jesus. The danger is not that we might lose our jobs but that we might lose our faith. Or at least the sharp edge of it. At least the desire to pursue the kingdom regardless of the cost. This is the real danger. Probably you can think of people who once were committed Christians and have been drawn over to the other side by the anxiety, or the allure, of the rat race. You may not feel susceptible to it now. But at age twenty-eight or thirty-three, with marriage or the birth of your first child, comes an incredible temptation to settle down, to allow the current of the culture to sweep you downstream and over the waterfall into the pool of self-absorption and petty pursuits.

■ *For Reflection*
Fruitful Labor
Think about your time in college.
- [ ] What kinds of academic work produced lasting fruit?
- [ ] What kinds of ministry effort produced lasting fruit?
- [ ] What other labor was deeply satisfying?

Think about your life in labor, forty to fifty hours a week, forty-eight to fifty weeks a year, for thirty-five to forty years. (That's 70,000-100,000 hours!)
- [ ] What kind of work can you do that you know will produce lasting fruit?

The Relationship Between Work and Needs
- [ ] How is your work related to the needs of others around you? For whom is God providing through you?
- [ ] How could your resources be freed up in order to better provide for the needs of others?

Vocation and Tents

☐ What do you know about yourself that would help you identify how you might best love God and love others through your work?

☐ It is difficult to know what personal factors led to Paul's choice of tentmaking as a job. What personal or preferential factors might influence your decision regarding work?

Models of Work and Ministry

There are many different ways to allocate your time and still be faithful disciples of Jesus, as the five examples in this chapter illustrate. Later I will give more attention to ministry and how to have your whole life mobilized to strive for God's kingdom. But as you consider the work that God has for you to do in his kingdom, consider now the spectrum of work-ministry options in light of your own gifts and interests.

☐ If you could allocate your time without regard to finances, where would you like to spend it?

☐ What extraneous pressures do you feel that impinge on your desires?

☐ Just as it is wrong to avoid giving your life to ministry because you don't think you would be provided for financially, it is also wrong to go into full-time ministry because you think that is the noble or mature Christian thing to do. Do these or other pressures make this a more difficult decision process?

☐ Do you feel vulnerable to any of the dangers mentioned above?

God's Values and the World's Values

The table on page 84 summarizes the contrasting set of values discussed in this chapter. This isn't meant to be taken as a simple contrast between all Christians and all non-Christians. As it is a summary, it is a form of stereotype. All of us, Christians as well as non-Christians, are at best a mixture of these values.

☐ How do your attitudes and values regarding work compare with those around you?

☐ What culturally significant values are you confronted with in your work setting?

☐ How might you interact in the work setting in ways that challenge values contrary to the gospel?

☐ In your life's intersection with the non-Christian culture, where is the danger to you personally? What values or assumptions of the culture are most alluring to you right now?

For Further Reading

Bernbaum, John A., and Simon M. Steer. *Why Work? Careers and Employment in Biblical Perspective.* Grand Rapids, Mich.: Baker Book House, 1986.

Harris, Janis Long. *Secrets of People Who Love Their Work.* Downers Grove, Ill.: InterVarsity Press, 1992.

Sine, Tom. *Wild Hope.* Waco, Tex.: Word, 1991.

5
Community
After College

The movie *The Big Chill* tells the story of a group of college friends who meet one weekend a decade after graduation. In the late sixties they had been campus radicals, but the film shows them in the early eighties. Most of the group members have bought into the system that they'd previously rejected and resisted. One of the two who never did accommodate to the system has killed himself; his funeral is the occasion for the group's gathering. The suicide of this man, who had been their friend and leader, has taken these folks by surprise and makes them review the direction their lives have taken the last several years. In each case they realize that they have made choices to live more comfortable, less radical lives. Yet they speak wistfully of the days when their lives had a greater urgency, a deeper sense of purpose, and their friendships had more substance. The warmth of their visionary days has been replaced by the chill of complacency.

One way to think about the social phenomenon depicted in *The Big Chill* is that it is the normal process of socialization in our society.

Idealistic, radical college students enter the "real world" and become upstanding citizens, defenders of the status quo, unwilling to rock the boat they now are sitting in comfortably.

Too often people speak about their time in a Christian college fellowship as the time when their faith was strongest and when ministry was most exciting. Even while still in college, many students wonder whether they'll be able to experience satisfying community and deep relationships with Christian brothers and sisters ever again. We come to doubt that what God has in store for us in the future is better than what we have already experienced.

A "big chill" is not inevitable for Christians graduating from college. We don't have to settle for the status quo. History is filled with the lives of people who went the other direction, for whom the flighty idealism of youth matured into a passionate drive to seek God's kingdom and minister in God's name. And for almost all of these people, one critical element sustained the commitment and passion needed to persevere. That element was Christian community.

This chapter and the next form a logical unit. First we'll consider the quality of relationships within a small fellowship group and look at key components of biblical community. Most people will find their fellowship group in a church context. A home fellowship group, a young adults Sunday-school class, a ministry team, a set of unstructured peer friendships—any of these could form the core of a functioning community within the context of a church. The next chapter, "Strategies for Church Involvement," focuses more on joining and contributing to the local church. Satisfaction in a church setting includes and is built on finding or developing a healthy small group, a community of growing disciples.

The Community of the King

The bulk of Jesus' teaching to his disciples cannot be understood outside the context of Christian community.[1] Jesus assumes that his disciples will follow him in groups. There is no provision for a one-on-one relationship with Jesus apart from other believers. The standard of quality of this life together is nothing less than the depth of

Jesus' love for his disciples:

> I give you a new commandment, that you love one another. Just as I have loved you, you also should love one another. By this everyone will know that you are my disciples, if you have love for one another. (John 13:34-35)

> This is my commandment, that you love one another as I have loved you. (John 15:12)

This type of love simply cannot be lived out within modern, convenient, culturally appropriate patterns of relationship. Jesus is not describing the "relationship chic" of our day, for which the primary tools are the appointment book and the telephone answering machine. Jesus calls for such a high quality of relationship in the community of believers that all those around will stand up and take notice. This will be a confirmation of Jesus' effective work in the world and a signpost to the kingdom of God.

Even Jesus' teaching on salvation does not give us the simple picture of an individual on his or her own being reconciled to God in a private prayer. Chapter three examined the story of the rich young man who approached Jesus with a sincere question, "Good Teacher, what must I do to inherit eternal life?" (see Mark 10:17-22). The man's question is a fundamental one: what is necessary for salvation?

Jesus' answer reveals his deep concern for this man. The man claimed to have obeyed the second tablet of the law (the commandments dealing with love for people), and Jesus did not contradict him. Yet the man lacked one thing. He had idolized money. In words that Jesus used elsewhere, he was not rich toward God (Luke 12:21). So Jesus told him to sell all his wealth, give the money to the poor and then come and join the band of followers who had already done essentially that. The man's relationship to God, according to Jesus' insight, could not be made right unless he gave up his wealth. But practically, the man could not have done this unless a community of God's people was ready to embrace him when he too became penniless and resourceless. Then he would learn along with the others the joy and freedom of dependence on God in the concrete form of the community.

Salvation and community for this man are integrally related. The man's problem, his wealth, kept him from experiencing a deep, loving trust relationship with God. But the solution to the man's problem would have drawn him into deep, loving trust relationships with his brothers and sisters, those who had also responded to Jesus' words. Jesus didn't intend for this wealthy young man to remain alone, isolated and alienated, hungry and destitute in a dreary life of asceticism. Jesus wanted him to come into the company of disciples, leaving behind anything that could get in the way. Jesus longed for him to discover the wealth and abundance available to all who cast their fortunes on the One from whom all blessings flow.

As the man left, Peter said to Jesus, "We've left everything to follow you," implying, "And what's in it for us?" Catching the implied question, Jesus reassured his concerned disciple. He stressed that whoever leaves behind family or property to follow him will receive a hundredfold in return, both family and property, in this life, though with persecutions (Mark 10:29-31). Now either this statement is indictable under truth-in-advertising laws or Jesus meant something other than blood relatives and title to real property held in our name. The only way to make sense of his statement is that Jesus' promises are fulfilled through the community of God's people. As people leave behind families to join the community of the King, they enter into a new family, with a hundredfold brothers and sisters and mothers. As people leave behind their own meager possessions, they enter into a wealth of community property, enjoying a hundred new places of hospitality and mutual generosity.

Community: God's Economy of Abundance

Jesus' economics are at variance with the economics of the "real world." The world's economic systems, whether capitalism or communism or any other "ism," operate on a fundamental principle of scarcity. In fact almost all current economic realities—greed, corruption, selfishness, bribes, cutthroat competition, international tariffs and trade barriers, mortgage interest rates, inflation, unemployment, real estate speculation, taxes, health insurance, and currency-exchange rate mechanisms—exist because of the notion of scarcity. Without scarcity of goods or capital to produce goods, none of these things would exist. Without scarcity there would be no motive for greed or corruption. Without scarcity competition would not be necessary. Of course scarcity entered the world when, as a result of the Fall, human work became toil. Jesus' ministry of redemption involves, in part, the redemption of the way we look at economic realities.

Consider again Jesus' words in Mark 10. He promises a hundredfold return on our investment if we leave behind family and lands for his sake in order to strive for the kingdom of God. How can he be so bold?

As the history of the church demonstrates, these words weren't mere empty promises. When Jesus says, "Heaven and earth will pass away, but my words will not pass away" (Mark 13:31), the immortal words he is referring to include his promise to Peter in Mark 10. Jesus spoke of and practiced an *economy of abundance,* not controlled by the laws of supply and demand but fueled by the unlimited resources of God, accessed through faith in him.[2]

We know that the early church experienced this same economy of abundance, practiced in Jerusalem shortly after Pentecost:

Now the whole group of those who believed were of one heart and soul, and no one claimed private ownership of any possessions, but everything they owned was held in common. With great power the apostles gave their testimony to the resurrection of the Lord Jesus, and great grace was upon them all. There was not a needy person among them, for as many as owned lands or houses sold them and brought the proceeds of what was sold. They laid it at the apostles' feet, and it was distributed to each as any had need. (Acts 4:32-35)

We also know that this economy of abundance was common practice throughout the early centuries of the church. The early apologists often pointed to Christians' extreme generosity and economic sharing as evidence of the work of God. Even the church's opponents observed that the church cared not only for its own poor but also for the pagan poor, and they credited this for the rapid spread of Christianity.[3]

What would it look like to live with the awareness of an economy of abundance today? It seems that one prerequisite is a light grip on our own possessions. In Acts no one claimed that anything was his or her own—they all shared in common. The result of this is that everyone felt wealthy, in that they all had access to anything they needed (Acts 4:34). We too can experience this same sort of wealth if we are willing to let go of *ownership* and replace it with a more biblical understanding of *stewardship*.

Sharing household resources. The household I used to live in owned a vacuum cleaner and a microwave oven. We were glad to allow members of the household next door to use these things, and that meant they didn't need to buy them. They received free use of our appliances. This left their household with more resources to use creatively. One of these creative enterprises was holding a weekly dinner to which any number of people could be invited. Drop-ins were always welcome. Soon a number of non-Christians as well as Christians became regular dinner guests. Their open-door policy was infectious: soon other Christian households of recent graduates began to have similar dinners, and the vision of the economy of abundance spread.

Buying a home. Two decades ago only a single average income allowed an individual or a couple to qualify for a loan to buy a modest house almost anywhere in the United States. Now in the most populated areas it takes at least two incomes (or one very substantial one) to qualify for a home loan. With the added hurdle of a down payment, home ownership has simply been priced out of reach for most recent graduates.[4] However, several sets of Christian friends of mine have been able to join together to make a down payment, qualify for a loan and afford a home. They are all living in more hospitable homes in more convenient neighborhoods than they would have been able to afford on their own. I know of couples with children buying property with singles or with childless couples. Even singles have purchased property together.

Of course one of the advantages of home ownership is the accumulation of equity in real property. It certainly beats sinking money into rent every month. But for many young couples or recent graduates from college, ownership would be impossible without a severe disruption of lifestyle. Purchasing property in community can make it possible and in fact can allow the participants to experience the economy of abundance, as they now have more room for hospitality, more resources for generosity and a relational abundance they would not experience living on their own. This is a case where current economic realities and the value of Christian community align to further the kingdom of God. Houses purchased in this way are more likely to be a witness to the world of the abundance of God's riches and his faithfulness to his promises. They are also more likely to produce the kind of experience we read about in Acts.

We can often observe a certain economy of abundance when people are in crisis. After a local disaster the entire community (and nation) responds to give aid to those in greatest need. If the disciples of Jesus all began to live out of the economy of abundance, what we now experience only in extreme times might become commonplace, and we would begin to see the world as Jesus did.

Components of Biblical Community

So far I have been using the word *community* in two senses. I want to give more specific shape to the definition of community, but let me begin here:

> *Community (concrete noun):*
> *a group of people with certain things in common.*
> *Community (abstract noun):*
> *the quality of sharing enjoyed by a group of people*
> *with certain things in common.*

Community can be built around any set of common circumstances, beliefs, values and preferences. This is the sense in which community is often used: a rural community is built around sharing a geographical location and quality-of-life preferences; a music community is built around a preference for a kind of music.

Consider your answer to the question, What things are so essential that if they are missing you don't have biblical community? I will look at three critical components: accountability, partnership and fellowship. Then we'll consider what a small group would be like if any one were missing. These elements are fundamental, yet not exhaustive, for an experience of true community.

Any Christian community exhibits these three aspects of commonality.

Christian community:
common commitment—accountability
common vision—partnership
common life—fellowship

These principles of Christian community are also fundamental for a healthy marriage or friendship. Aristotle's definition of friendship used the same three components, stated slightly differently. He said that friends must enjoy each other, be useful to one another and share a commitment to "the good."[5]

Accountability. Skim over Hebrews 3:12—4:1. Here the writer of this letter expresses concern for his readers because they are suffering from complacency. People are assuming that once they have begun to follow Christ, God's blessings are assured and they can coast. So the writer says, in effect, "Take care; we must hold fast until the end." Perseverance is critical.

The message of Hebrews is a message for us as well. We are told to exhort each other "as long as it is called 'today' " (3:13). In other words, we are never to stop exhorting each other. When tomorrow comes, it will still be called "today," so continue to exhort each other. This is a daily discipline, not one to be practiced only in very rare and severe circumstances. The author is aware of the danger and the possibility of falling away from the living God, and mutual exhortation is one way to keep people on track. It is an exercise of love to exhort someone rather than watch them fall into sin.

The "deceitfulness of sin" (3:13) is dangerous. It isn't that we are all trying to get away with as little as possible. We may want to follow

God, but sin is often hard to recognize. Since sin doesn't advertise itself as sin, we slide into it before we realize it.

Furthermore, we are warned of a hardened heart, an "evil, unbelieving heart" (3:12). Now, if we faced a choice between an evil, unbelieving heart and a soft heart toward God, it would be easy. The problem is that the hardened heart doesn't just show up one day. Our once-soft hearts are calcified slowly, as a result of a long series of daily choices. It comes on little by little through small disappointments, petty frustrations and "harmless" but faithless decisions.

The passage stresses the necessity of thinking about our discipleship in terms of "today." We all have a tendency to live our lives with God either in the past (focusing on the status we have achieved as disciples and what we've accomplished) or in the future ("Next year I will take these steps of faithfulness," or "I will go to the mission field in five years"). Our discipleship must be rooted in *today.* And we need brothers and sisters who are willing to challenge us when our "today" actions don't align with our convictions, our faithful choices from the past or our God-directed vision for the future.

Notice as well that little credit is given to any individual for being able to remain undeceived by sin. Even Israelites who saw miracles in Egypt and in the desert fell away. The biblical picture of human nature is that we tend to fall away and to be deceived by sin. While a few may be able to remain faithful while all around them have fallen away, isolation is not the likely context of faithful discipleship.

Finally, the author speaks with urgency. Imagine that a parent of a young child notices the child sitting in the middle of the street. How would the parent respond? In even tones—"Uh, Timmy, I just think it'd be safer if you got out of the road"? Quietly and patiently—"Timmy, you might want to play in the grass and not on the street"? No, the parent would snap into action, yelling, "Timmy, get out of the street!" and rushing to snatch the child up. The urgency and the shout are signs of love, not anger. The parent simply wants to see young Timmy survive and grow up.

Some Christians might argue, "That kind of discipline is necessary for children, and parents have a responsibility to administer it, but I am not responsible in the same way for the decisions of other adult Christians." Unfortunately, because of the intense individualism of Western culture, that kind of thinking is rampant and unquestioned in the church. But it is not the thinking of Jesus or of his disciples. While we cannot force people to make faithful choices, we *can* exhort and encourage them and warn them of the consequences of sin (see 2 Timothy 4:2). We are also commanded to forgive them and receive them when they acknowledge their sin. And when the tables are turned, we are to receive exhortation with an understanding of the intention of love and concern behind it.

Partnership. Romans 16 is an interesting chapter. You probably haven't heard many sermons preached on it. It is the concluding section of Paul's letter to the church in Rome. Paul wrote his letter as a means of introduction to the church there, probably before he had ever been to Rome. Chapter 16 reveals a web of close relationships that is remarkable, given that he had never been in Rome. He had met people in Ephesus and they ended up in Rome; he had met people in Corinth and they ended up in Rome. It is clear that these people were important to Paul and he wanted them to know it.

In this chapter Paul mentions many fellow workers, former partners who had worked with him in ministry. These partners are like family to him. Among them Paul lists both men and women: Phoebe, Prisca, Aquila, Andronicas, Junia, Mary, Tryphaena, Tryphosa. Also he mentions the partners who are with him when he writes the letter: Timothy, Lucius, Jason, Sosipater. Tertius is writing the letter for Paul, who has bad eyesight. Paul is living with Gaius.

Paul is not teaching on partnership; he is just demonstrating that he has lots of partners. Obviously this passage isn't high in theological content. And yet we definitely get a clear message: Paul is grateful for all of his partnerships, and he is very aware of his need for others. (Prisca and Aquila even risked their lives for him.) He values his fellow workers and has many of them, both men and women. This famed (and probably misunderstood) "chauvinist" consistently puts women in a place of being coapostles and coworkers with himself.

Given my discussion of accountability, we might infer that the main reason we need other people in our lives is that we are sinful and in need of correction. But even from the beginning God designed humans to be in community: "Then the LORD God said, 'It is not good that the man should be alone; I will make him a helper as his partner' " (Genesis 2:18).

It is not good for us to be alone, and God gives us partners in one another. The human need for partnership isn't merely a concession to the fact that we are sinful people and can't follow God faithfully on our own. Even before the Fall God recognized that it is not good for humans to be alone, so he created an ecology that requires partnership for survival. In Eve, God gives Adam most fundamentally not a romantic interest, not a sexual mate, but a *partner*.

In our society marriage seems like the only real model of partnership (and often not a good one), but certainly Scripture presents many other kinds of partnership. In most of Paul's letters, he greets people by name and writes with a group. He sends people to take letters to churches. Often we skip over these portions of his letters, yet they illustrate how important partnership was to Paul. He could not even write a letter without a partner, let alone plant a church.

Fellowship. Finally, look at Acts 2:42-47. Here Luke, the author of Acts, describes the life of the young Jerusalem church in the first weeks after its explosive beginning at Pentecost. Miracles were commonplace; miraculous healings and miraculous generosity characterized the church. People cared for the needy, ate in homes together and gathered in the temple to worship God. They had everything in common: possessions, homes, meals, life. They saw the mighty power of God and experienced his presence.

Furthermore, you get the sense that it was through the appeal and integrity of their life together that people were added to the church day by day. What the apostles taught about Jesus the church lived out. The preaching called people to a lifestyle, and their fellowship was the daily experience of it. The harmony between Jesus' teaching and the lives of his disciples had a tremendous impact. Their corporate life attracted attention; outsiders were first impressed and curious, then interested, then involved, finally committed. God's power was released as people lived in this way. Daily they saw evidence of God in their midst.

Apart from the gospel it is impossible for people to live in close community and experience deep fellowship. In *The Great Divorce* C. S. Lewis gives an insightful if fanciful picture of hell—a place, he says, where people cannot tolerate one another. He pictures a great, flat plain extending to infinity in all directions. Here people are constantly moving away from one another in order to escape the demands of relationship. Precisely because in this hell there is no room for forgiveness and reconciliation, there is no possibility of society or community. The "not good" of solitary human life of Genesis 2:18 becomes Lewis's vision of hell. His description is quite close to the scene the apostle Paul depicts of those without Christ in Ephesians 2:11-14: alienated, separated, without hope or God, far off.

But with the good news of Jesus Christ, this cosmic alienation has been reversed. The key ingredient is forgiveness. We who have been forgiven huge debts by God can easily forgive the trivial impositions of others (Matthew 18:21-35). The dividing walls of hostility that separate us have been torn down through Christ's death (Ephesians 2:14-19). This makes it possible for Christians to live in committed relationships over many years. Forgiveness is the key to longevity and happiness in marriage, in ministry partnerships, in household living situations, in friendships of all kinds. It is what makes it possible to say that life in God's kingdom, with his people, is actually "sweeter as the days go by."

Having considered a few of the many biblical arguments for these fundamental components of community, now let's think about what each of these might look like in the practice of a functioning church fellowship, small group or household community.

Common Commitment: Accountability

A small group desiring to enjoy Christian community will be built on a set of common convictions about how to relate to God and to one another. Various small groups will interpret what it means to love God and love one another differently. Some (monastic orders) may call their members to poverty, chastity and obedience, while others may simply expect that their members will pray regularly and get along well. The shape of the commitments will be likely to reflect the role of Scripture in the small group. The common commitments may be in written form, like a covenant. Or perhaps they are simply the body of convictions the group holds.

Accountability, then, implies a recognition of and commitment to the truth. We must acknowledge that the truth about God can be known (although never perfectly), and we must acknowledge the truth about ourselves. If we are unable to affirm anything as true, or if we deny the truth about ourselves, accountability is meaningless.

This means we are going to share with our small group the struggles and temptations we face, asking for help and prayer. We will also confess our sins and failings, hearing in response Nathan's words to David: "The LORD has put away your sin" (2 Samuel 12:13). Accountability introduces a higher authority for the group. A critic might say, "You are judging people." But a group member can respond, "We are all under authority. It is not that you are under *my* authority, but that we are all under the authority of Scripture as we understand it."

Therefore a requisite for accountability in community is submission—to one another (Ephesians 5:21), to leadership (Romans 13:1; Hebrews 13:17) and to clear teachings of Scripture (2 Timothy 3:16-17). Unwillingness to submit to the accountability of the community is the most certain way of effectively eliminating yourself from community. If unwillingness to submit is a characteristic of the entire community, it will neither offer nor receive effective accountability.

This is not to set the accountability structure of such a group in opposition to the leadership structure of a church. Most often the leadership of a community will be recognized lay church leadership. Small groups and other forms of community will need to ensure that their leaders themselves are accountable to others in the church, church board, eldership or pastoral staff. For successful community, healthy accountability structures must be combined with each person's humble submission to authority. This is difficult for many of us.

Economic sharing. The members of one community household decided to pool their incomes and pay expenses from a common bank account. (Owners of assets acquired before the community formed kept that ownership.) This level of community is called "economic koinonia." (The Greek word *koinōnia* is the New Testament word for "partnership" or "sharing.") One commitment the members of this household made to one another was that none of them would spend more than ten dollars of discretionary money without consulting the others, if possible the entire household, beforehand. Their goal was a form of simplicity, calling the household members to be conscientious and disciplined in their spending.

The group embraced the challenge and welcomed the mutual accountability that would make this kind of arrangement work. Yet the requirement was not legalistically conceived: to spend more than ten dollars was not considered sin, and each household member enjoyed the generosity of the others by being allowed to spend money for nonnecessities, such as going out to eat with friends, taking someone to a movie, buying a CD. But the household was able to help each member become more accountable for the way each spent money. This was no small thing in a highly materialistic culture. Members of the community said that just knowing they would need to justify their desire to spend money prevented most frivolous expenditures.

It would be difficult to overemphasize the importance of *common* in this section's title, "Common Commitments." Accountability means nothing if you ask someone to hold you to some value that you do not share. And we will hardly welcome accountability if people try to exhort us to live as we have no intention of living. This is why any thriving community must examine Scripture regularly together. Common Scripture study allows us to call people to commitment to the authoritative Word of God.

Common Vision: Partnership in Ministry

It is critical for vital Christian community that the members be involved in ministry together. Ministry gives purpose to the common commitments and paces the development of the community as a whole. Here is how Paul speaks of the importance of ministry to the overall goal of the Christian community, the body of Christ:

> The gifts he gave were that some would be apostles, some prophets, some evangelists, some pastors and teachers, to equip the saints for the work of ministry, for building up the body of Christ, until all of us come to the unity of the faith and of the knowledge of the Son of God, to maturity, to the measure of the full stature of Christ, . . . from whom the whole body, . . . as each part is working properly, promotes the body's growth in building itself up in love. (Ephesians 4:11-13, 16)

Paul affirms that the purpose of a body of believers is to bring every member into full maturity in the faith. His vision is that we all grow together to measure up to nothing less than the stature of Christ.[6] The church's goal is to complete the discipleship process for each member and to mature as a body. Accomplishing this involves equipping every member for the work of ministry. If the members are working properly and working together, then the healthy body will grow up into the fullness of Christ.

Ministry, as Paul uses the word here, means both ministry *to* the saints and ministry *of* the saints to those who do not yet believe. The building up of the body of Christ involves both qualitative development and numerical growth as new members are added to the faith. A functioning community of Christians yields both the pastoral development of the believers and evangelistic fruit. In fact, these aspects of ministry are complementary. As younger Christians are called to care for and witness to others, they grow in their faith as well.

In college you may have experienced a community that called its members into ministry. Your college fellowship geared up for ministry, especially at certain times of the year: outreach to new students during the fall, perhaps a campuswide evangelistic event, weekend retreats. At each of these times the mission of your college group was well defined and each member of the community joined in working toward the overall goal. As each part was working properly, the entire community grew, in joy and love for one another as well as numerically.

Common vision is critical. As you consider small group involvement in a postcollege setting, perhaps you feel little hope for a common vision for ministry. If each member of the community has a particular vision with little coordination or partnership throughout the whole, over time the pull of those different visions may sap and undermine the community as a whole. This does not mean that everyone will do the same thing, play the same role or contribute the same gifts. But even with a diversity of gifts, they all contribute toward the same goal.

Household community. A group of college graduates are interested in living together in a form of household community. Early in the discussions the group should consider the vision of their community. What is the area of need to which the community is called to minister? Perhaps it is the young-adult age group of a local church or the youth of a nearby inner-city neighborhood. Perhaps the group senses a call to go overseas, to become a team involved in crosscultural ministry.

Many common visions are worth pursuing. Different communities will pursue different visions. Yet it is critical that a community household have a common vision. This vision will determine subsequent decisions:

☐ Where should we look for housing?

☐ Who will be the main recipients of the household's hospitality?

☐ What other resources and partners will we need to seek out to pursue our vision?

Common Life: Fellowship

The common life of a small group is perhaps its most visible feature. This is often what makes a community either attractive or oppressive, depending on how it functions.

It takes time to build community. There is no shortcut; there is no bureaucratic or institutional replacement for simply spending time together. A household of people must decide to share meals and set aside regular time for one another if their living arrangement is to be Christian community. Otherwise it can feel like a hotel, with corresponding low relational expectations. One indication of the "hotelization" of a household is that people treat common areas as if they expect a maid to do all the cleaning!

Of course any group will need to allow community to develop—it won't exist fully formed immediately. In a healthy and growing small group, people are increasingly willing to alter their priorities so that they can spend quality time together. Some may decide that the value of a weekly meal together is worth the extra effort of cooking and hosting. Or someone may decide to buy a car in order to be able to spend more time with other members in their homes.

Small group community. A group of recent graduates attending the same church grow dissatisfied with the level of sharing they experience in their small group. Living together is not an option, though two pairs of roommates are in the group. What can they do to build a greater sense of fellowship and deeper community in their group?

It is certainly possible to experience deep community between people not living under the same roof. Because of their common desire to grow, small group members will probably want to spend time together in a variety of contexts:

□ *Scripture study.* This can be a fundamental element of all three commonalities: common commitments, common vision and common life. Giving priority to Scripture study will add depth to the group's fellowship life.

□ *Worship.* Corporate worship as a small group lifts our sights from our own "to do" lists to set them on God, who calls us into relationship with himself as well as with one another. Worship is especially meaningful in a group that is able to confess sins to one another, receive forgiveness and be reconciled. Worship reminds us that we all stand in need of the same grace and forgiveness from God through Jesus Christ.

□ *Meals.* The early church in Acts was characterized by "breaking bread together" in each other's homes. Much of Jesus' teaching happened in the context of meals in people's homes. With a little intentionality, meals can be fruitful times. Shared meals give room for relationships to form and deepen, and in that setting group members can welcome guests into their fellowship.

□ *Celebrations.* God commanded the people of Israel to celebrate and commemorate certain events in their past, reminding themselves of

God's faithfulness to them throughout their history. A small group will gain much by fostering this same spirit of celebration and remembrance. Traditional holidays, birthdays and anniversaries of community milestones are all worth celebrating. Celebrations also offer avenues for a variety of gifts to be used for the benefit of the whole.

☐ *Movies.* If thoughtfully planned, a night at a theater or at home with a video can foster community. While most videos are pointless, dozens of movies do raise important issues and are worth watching in community. Movies, for better or for worse, are chief carriers of the values of our culture. Better to watch them in community with a critical eye than to absorb their messages unchallenged.

☐ *Road trips.* Jesus often took his disciples on the road or across the lake in extended trips away from his home base. When we are out of our home environment, relational patterns change and friendships can grow more quickly. So weekend retreats are effective for giving a church or fellowship group a greater sense of community. But beyond the familiar retreat, consider other forms of road trips: week-long vacations together, camping trips, short-term crosscultural missions trips, or tours to visit ministries, churches, communities or missionaries.

One year I led a small group with three graduating students, Steve, Brian and Seth. We all learned much that year as we met weekly to pray and share about our lives. After their graduation we decided to take a three-week trip across the United States, from California to New York City, then visiting Washington, D.C., Jackson, Mississippi, and other cities. We wanted an adventure, but we also were interested in visiting thriving inner-city ministries.

Daily God stunned us by showing us his vision and hope for the city. We spent much of our travel time debriefing on what we had seen. Each day our relationships with one another deepened, and we were excited to consider our future partnership. The four of us chose to live together the following year, continuing in ministry together and growing in our understanding and experience of Christian community.

Community in Equilibrium

Now that we've examined three components of Christian community, let's consider how these components fit together, using the diagram below.

I call this a force diagram because the three commonalities discussed above can be understood as forces producing a dynamic equilibrium in a healthy community. Accountability is the inward force, partnership in ministry is the outward force, and fellowship is the binding force, like glue holding it all together.

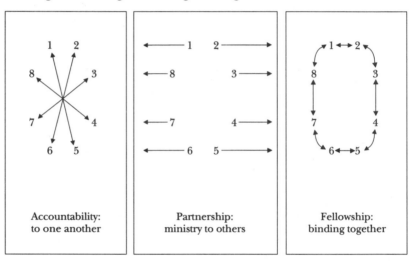

| Accountability: to one another | Partnership: ministry to others | Fellowship: binding together |

What happens when one or more of these forces is underdeveloped or not present? Without all three forces in balance, the community falls out of equilibrium; it is unstable and will not long endure. Depending on which force is missing, the community may fly apart, splinter off or cave in on itself. In fact, all communities have weaknesses that if unaddressed may make them unstable. This is why so many marriages, friendships, households and churches split apart after a time. We want to aim for community with vibrant health and longevity.[7]

The point is not to limit our definition of biblical community to a particular incarnation or even a particular mix of these three ingredients. Some successful communities are stronger in some of the elements than others, and that's fine. And hopefully any community you are a part of will grow and develop over time. The examples discussed below are the extreme cases: if you recognize a lack of some element in your small group or church, you may be able to work toward change and a more healthy balance of the components of community.

What would "community" be like without each of these three commonalities?

Without accountability. Consider first a small group that has a strong common life and an outward focus in ministry yet offers its members no accountability. Members may enjoy being together and are involved in ministry together, but they aren't deeply involved in each other's lives. Because accountability is the most inward of the commonalities, a group without it can still look like a great community on the outside. At least for a while.

But none of the members get the help they need. Caught up in the desires of the world, some people fall into temptation and sin, especially sexual immorality and materialism. Others are broken people whose brokenness is not apparent in ten-minute chats after the Sunday-school class or the small group meeting. They remain in patterns of pain and discouragement because they are not given the accountability they need to take steps out of an unhealthy way of life.[8]

God provides for a small group in part through the spiritual and physical resources of its members. If ministry and fellowship continue without accountability, these resources will be depleted over time, just as a car eventually breaks down if no one ever bothers to put oil in it. A healthy group must have accountability in some form, or it will be impoverished over time and will hollow out and fly apart.

Without partnership in ministry. Now consider a small group with great fellowship and mutual accountability but no partnership in ministry. The small group is ingrown. In a high school we would call it a clique; in a church we might call it a social club. All of its energy is focused into the group; none is focused outward. Members lack vision for evangelism or service.

A small group without ministry is also unstable. There is no ultimate purpose in being together. Think about what happens to cliques in

108

FOLLOWING JESUS IN THE "REAL WORLD"

high school. Without an outward focus they collapse or splinter apart.[9] All the energy that people have for relationships is turned inward and becomes judgmental, producing gossip, backbiting and factions. Eventually such groups either divide over trivial issues or disintegrate as members drift apart.

Without fellowship. Here we consider the rare example of a community with accountability and partnership in ministry but no fellowship. This is the least attractive form of pseudocommunity, resembling the stereotype of a marines boot camp. Such an outward-focused, mission-driven group is often fairly hierarchically organized. Involvement in this "community" might center on high-intensity relationships with a "discipler" and eventually with one's disciples.

Here people are "tough loved" but they aren't soft loved. Group members may begin to feel that their lives are being inordinately monitored and arbitrarily judged. Accountability can produce tension; without the warm love of fellowship the tension can break up the group. Members are supposed to be in ministry to outsiders, but this kind of community is not very attractive to invite people to. It becomes exclusively task-oriented, a situation that is self-defeating. Since the "task" is advancing the kingdom, and the kingdom is principally relational, we cannot advance the kingdom without loving people, especially those in our own small group.

Finally, we can summarize the three commonalities as follows:

Community involves . . .	Common . . .	Fundamental quality	Without it a group is characterized by . . .
Accountability	Commitments	Truth	Sin and hypocrisy
Partnership	Vision	Mission	Lack of cohesion
Fellowship	Life	Love	Lack of joy

Implications

Let me emphasize several specific implications of the understanding of community I have been building in this chapter.

Community households. A decision to live together as Christians doesn't make community. Moving into a house together or renting an apartment with a couple of Christians doesn't even ensure common life, let alone common vision and common commitments. A group of people who decide to live together may not be ready for the commonalities of community, but then it is probably best not to call the situation Christian community. Set realistic expectations.

But if you want to experience deeper community, mobilize your resources to make it happen. It will mean making your time available for common life. It will mean making your relationships open to common commitments and accountability. It will mean talking through what you want to pursue so as to make common vision and partnership a reality. If these things are all present, you should have a lot of hope that your housing situation will yield Christian community.

Nonhousehold community. Just as a decision to live together doesn't ensure community, neither does a separate living situation preclude it. In both situations you will need to make intentional choices in order to deepen relationships and pursue the components of community discussed in this chapter.

Several people not living in the same household or apartment desire to develop community. If they are willing to make priority decisions to achieve their goal, they have many creative options. For example, they could arrange a rotation of meals so that they eat together two or three nights a week, with their small group meeting for Bible study, prayer and accountability on one of these nights. The economy of scale involved in cooking less frequently for more people could actually counter the added transportation time involved, making this option *more* time-efficient. Another of the joint-meal nights could be an open time to invite other friends, hang out, go out to movies or enjoy a video.

The only thing getting in the way of the development of community is time, and since everyone has the same amount of time in absolute terms, the only thing preventing people from making the choice to spend time together is a difference of priorities. As people begin to experience and increasingly to value community, they will be willing to make choices to pursue it more.

First steps. Perhaps you are tempted to think, "The boat has left the dock; I wish I had been ready." No timetable governs progress toward postcollege Christian community. The point is to get moving. If you are attracted to the kind of community described in this chapter, take steps to move toward it. Be the person to make this happen. You cannot create community alone, but you certainly can thwart or reject it when it comes along.

Consider asking your small group to take a weekend away together, perhaps at a retreat center or Christian conference. Try to include both meaningful content and fun time. Plan as a community to interact with Scripture in a significant way, to begin to develop common commitments to which you can be held accountable. Look at the book of Ephesians to see what Paul says about the nature of the church. That will challenge your understanding of what it means to be in relationships with other Christians.

"I'm in! How about you?" Chances are you know some people who would also be attracted to a deeper experience of community. Perhaps you already have a small group that meets weekly, but you know it could be much more. Perhaps you can say to the others, "I'm in! How about you?" By "in" I don't mean physically in—that is, moving into a house somewhere. Even more important is the emotional "in": "I'm willing to make priority decisions around you guys." You can say "I'm in" and invite others to join you, to make risky choices to be faithful to what God wants for you as individuals and as a community.

Leadership and community. Broad ownership is key to a functioning community. Yet leadership is also crucial; leadership gifts must somehow be recognized, and group members must work to submit to leaders. Different leadership roles will emerge: some people may be gifted for teaching, others for pastoral care, others for visionary leadership, others for administrative decision-making. Different forms of community will work out the leadership structure differently, but the ability of a community to recognize *and submit to* leadership will, to a great extent, determine its viability. The inability to submit to leadership is often what kills churches, households and ministry teams.

Think about how your community recognizes and empowers leadership. How easily do people take on leadership, authority and decision-making roles within your community? How valued and appreciated are those roles?

Is there someone to whom the leaders of your community are also accountable—your pastor or church leaders, for example? This kind of relationship can give community members greater confidence in the wisdom and direction of those in leadership.

The evolution of community. It is critical to enter into a small group expecting that community will take time to grow. Yet we also must expect that community will take different forms at different times in our lives. Marriage and children will change the nature of our experience of community with others. When such changes occur, we may be tempted to one of two responses. We may be frustrated when these life-stage changes affect our small group experience of community. Or anticipating the inevitable changes, we may reserve ourselves and not pursue depth with others.

Yet if we have entered into deep and satisfying community before these changes occur, we are more likely to continue to value community, to make choices to pursue it and thus to experience new rewards. For example, my wife and I recently became parents. Our experience of community has changed, but we are enjoying new benefits: our community has given us tremendous help in the care of our infant son.

*   *   *

This chapter began with a look at a secular film's depiction of a warm college-based community that experienced a chill after many years. Another secular film depicts a very different kind of community. *Brother Son, Sister Moon* is Franco Zeffirelli's beautiful recounting of the story of Saint Francis. Francis's story is the reverse of those in *The Big Chill.* He was reckless and wild in his youth, but not one to resist the status quo at all: he went off to the war of his day, unlike the radicals of the 1960s who protested the Vietnam War. Yet illness and a subsequent conversion brought about a total repentance, and he became idealistic and radical—as radical as any radicals today. Other young people, also disenchanted with their society and the hypocrisy in the church, joined Francis in his efforts to live by Jesus' model and to take Jesus' teachings seriously. It was the community of those who chose to live together that made it possible and attractive to pursue a radical lifestyle. The Franciscan orders grew to have a dramatic impact on the life and health of the church of the late Middle Ages.

This is the kind of experience we hope to have, binding our lives together with others in Jesus' name. We will grow as disciples of Jesus as his first disciples did, listening to his teaching and submitting to it in a group. We will learn to love God and one another in a community ignited by God's Spirit, stoked by God's Word and guided by the vision of the advance of God's kingdom.

■ For Reflection
The Community of the King
☐ As you anticipate making difficult choices to follow Jesus after college, do you have a community of disciples that will help you remain faithful to Jesus?

☐ If yes, how can they tangibly be of help? In what areas of discipleship do your brothers and sisters provide encouragement?

☐ If no, how can you discover, join or develop such a community?

Community: God's Economy of Abundance
☐ How much are you aware of God's "economy of abundance"?

☐ Do you live as though you believe God is generous and his resources are abundant and available to you through God's people? Or do you live with a scarcity mentality, acquiring and protecting possessions as a priority? Or somewhere in between?

☐ How could you take steps to move toward a greater reliance on God's economy? What form of Christian community could help you do this?

Common Commitment: Accountability
☐ Do you have friends with whom you already share struggles and confess sin? Thank God for these relationships.

☐ If not, do you have friends with whom you could begin to do this?

☐ What would it cost you? What would be the potential benefits?

Common Vision: Partnership in Ministry
☐ Reflect on potential partners with whom you share vision for ministry.
☐ What are your strengths as a partner? What gets in the way?

Common Life: Fellowship
☐ Do you find that recent changes to your life and schedule have made it easier to spend time in fellowship with your community or potential community, or more difficult?
☐ How can you make priority decisions that will help you and others make fellowship more satisfying?

For Further Reading
Bonhoeffer, Dietrich. *Life Together.* Translated by John Doberstein. New York: Harper & Row, 1954.
Lohfink, Gerhard. *Jesus and Community.* Philadelphia: Fortress, 1984.
Snyder, Howard. *The Community of the King.* Downers Grove, Ill.: InterVarsity Presss, 1977.

6
Strategies for Church Involvement

The film *The Dream Team* is an imaginative if unlikely comedy about four patients in a mental hospital and the psychiatrist who leads their group-therapy sessions. The psychiatrist gets the daring idea to take these four guys to a Yankees baseball game to help them to loosen up and relax with him and one another. Through a freak coincidence, and unfortunately for his plan, the psychiatrist ends up witnessing a murder. Having been beaten up by the criminals, he is eventually discovered and taken away in an ambulance, while the four patients obediently stay in their car.

In the bizarre chain of events that follows, this group of semifunctioning, mutually hostile adults eventually come to realize that they must rely on one another and work together in order to find their doctor and, as it turns out, save his life. They face enormous obstacles (they are wanted by the police for their doctor's beating and for the murder he witnessed), but in the end—and to great comic effect—each of the members of the "dream team" uses his particular gifts and quirks to find and save the doctor. The result is their best therapy ever, as each comes to understand his own gifts and also his need for the others. Through the ordeal they all make progress in their emotional growth and healing.

Though it is hardly flattering to say it, part of what I enjoy about that film is that it reminds me of the church. Not the Church Triumphant but the church at Fifth and Main. Not the Church Universal but the church particular. A group of people who without the Spirit of God in their midst might be at each other's throats. A group of people some of whom can barely function in society. A group of people with little quirks that make them very funny, if you could stand back and see them from the right angle. Yet somehow, through the grace and power of God, this odd collection of people, when they come together, are called to be the very incarnation of Jesus on the earth. And as they struggle to become what they are called to become, each grows and experiences much-needed healing.

Unfortunately, no one really wants to identify with such a weird assortment of people. In the movie each member of the group thought that he didn't belong there and it was the others who had problems. If you have recently graduated from college, you too may also be tempted to view the church (that is, the one you attended last Sunday) as a group of strange individuals very much different from yourself. And yet everything in Scripture tells us that if we are to follow Jesus we *will* participate in his body, the church. That church is not the church invisible but rather the church all-too-visible, the one down the block with all the sinners and hypocrites in it. And if we are honest with ourselves, we fit right in at such a church!

Models of the Church

Before we consider practical strategies for church involvement, we need to examine the nature of the church. What is it supposed to be? The answer to this will help us to know how to relate to the church. In a short book on the nature of the church, *The Outward Bound*, Vernard Eller uses two contrasting images to describe how the church sees itself.

A *commissary is an institution* which has been *commissioned* to *dispense* particular goods, services, or benefits to a select *constituency*. The commissary church, then, sees itself primarily as an institution, a *divine institution franchised by God.* God has stocked the institution with a supply of heavenly graces (Bible truths, correct theology, the sacraments, etc.) which the clerical proprietors, through proper transaction, can disburse to the customers. The measure of a commissary, it follows, lies in the legality of its franchise, the warranty of its goods, and the authorization of its personnel.

A *caravan*, on the other hand, is something entirely different. It is a group of people banded together to make *common cause* in seeking a *common destination*. . . . The being of a caravan lies not in any signed and sealed authorization but *in the way it functions.* Its validity lies not in its apparatus but in the performance of its caravaners—each and every one of them. A caravan is a caravan only as long as it is making progress—or at least striving to make progress. Once the caravaners stop, dig in, or count themselves as having arrived, they no longer constitute a caravan.[1]

Eller says that the early church understood itself as a caravan; the people of God were banded together on a trip to the City of God. The book of Hebrews makes a clear statement of this. Emphasizing the continuity of faith in Jesus with authentic Judaism, the author reviews the lives of many Old Testament heroes and heroines of faith:

All of these died in faith without having received the promises, but from a distance they saw and greeted them. They confessed that they were strangers and foreigners on the earth, for people who speak in this way make it clear that they are seeking a homeland. If they had been thinking of the land that they had left behind, they would have had opportunity to return. But as it is, they desire a better country, that is, a heavenly one. Therefore God is not ashamed to be called their God; indeed, he has prepared a city for them. (Hebrews 11:13-16)

We can also understand the tension between Eller's two models of the church through the conflict between Jesus and the Pharisees. The religious establishment of Jesus' day had a "commissary" understanding of Jewish religion, especially of the synagogues and the temple. According to them, Jesus was not an authorized purveyor of the spiritual goods available in their system; he seemed to set up a competitive shop where anyone, including *nonauthorized* customers, could receive forgiveness or healing—even on the sabbath day, when such things were not supposed to happen. Jesus called people to follow him and hence to join one another in doing so. His caravan took on a literal form as he walked ahead of the pack of fearful and amazed disciples on the way to Jerusalem (Mark 10:32). After Jesus' death and resurrection, he reiterates his initial call to his first disciple: "Follow me!" (John 21:19, 22). The caravan doesn't stop until we all arrive in the heavenly city.

In Ephesians 4 Paul describes a clear vision for the church involving both "common cause" and "common destination." Paul depicts a caravan of people who thrive and grow and progress together as each contributes. Paul expresses the common destination of the church in various ways:

☐ "until all of us come to the unity of the faith and of the knowledge of the Son of God, to maturity, to the measure of the full stature of Christ" (v. 13)

☐ "we must grow up in every way into him who is the head, into Christ" (v. 15)

☐ "promotes the body's growth in building itself up in love" (v. 16)

He likewise expresses the "common cause" of the church:

☐ "there is one body and one Spirit, just as you were called to the one hope of your calling" (v. 4)

☐ "the gifts he gave . . . to equip the saints for the work of ministry, for building up the body of Christ" (vv. 11-12)

☐ "the whole body, joined and knit together by every ligament" (v. 16)

☐ "as each part is working properly" (v. 16)

The church Paul describes sounds pretty exciting! The leaders are gifted in training the saints for ministry. That ministry grows and develops the entire body, both qualitatively and numerically. Growth, speaking the truth, love, each member working properly—wow! Paul

118

FOLLOWING JESUS IN THE "REAL WORLD"

envisions an attractive dynamic of change; this is what the church is supposed to look like.

The image of a caravan can be connected to the image of community developed in chapter five of this book. A caravan is a *community on the move*. Some communities may be tempted to settle down, becoming rooted, permanent and perhaps complacent. But the caravan community of disciples will continue to take risks to follow Jesus to the heavenly city. This perspective profoundly affects our lifestyle choices. (See chapter seven.)

We may be tempted to assume that certain denominations will show up at certain locations on the spectrum of commissary to caravan. Yet the reality is that God is at work in churches all over. The most historically institutional church in the West is the Roman Catholic Church, but even that is changing. Avery Dulles, a Jesuit theologian, reflects on this change:

> Vatican Council II in its Constitution on the Church made ample use of the models of the body of Christ and the Sacrament, but its dominant model was rather that of the People of God. This paradigm focused attention on the Church as a network of interpersonal relationships, on the Church as community. This is still the dominant model for many Roman Catholics who consider themselves progressives and invoke the teaching of Vatican II as their authority.[2]

God is at work renewing his church, bringing new life into structures that have become institutionalized. God desires that his church be a "people of the Way," as the early church was called. And God sends his Spirit to urge the church forward.

If the caravan model more closely reflects God's desire for his church than the commissary model, that has implications for us as participants in it. We are not members of churches the way people are members of discount shopping clubs. Membership in the church looks more like membership on a football team. Our fortunes rise and fall as a team, and we all must work together to fulfill our purpose. The rest of this chapter focuses on the practical implications of this model.

Take Your Place in the Body

What are you doing when you join a church? Why should you join one? You may take the answers to these questions for granted, but if finding a church after college proves difficult, the questions become relevant. To find a clue to the answer, consider the pivotal event in the apostle Paul's life:

> With [pursuit of the Christians] in mind, I was traveling to Damascus with the authority and commission of the chief priests, when at midday along the road . . . I saw a light from heaven, brighter than the sun, shining around me and my companions. When we had all fallen to the ground, I heard a voice saying to me in the Hebrew language, "Saul, Saul, why are you persecuting me? It hurts you to kick against the goads." I asked, "Who are you, Lord?" The Lord answered, "I am Jesus whom you are persecuting. But get up and stand on your feet; for I have appeared to you for this purpose, to appoint you to serve and testify to the things in which you have seen me and to those in which I will appear to you. I will rescue you from your people and from the Gentiles—to whom I am sending you to open their eyes so that they may turn from darkness to light and from the power of Satan to God, so that they may receive forgiveness of sins and a place among those who are sanctified by faith in me." (Acts 26:12-18)

In this passage Paul recounts his conversion in his defense before King Agrippa. Prior to this he has told Agrippa that as the Pharisee Saul, he had been a furious persecutor of Christians, zealous to see them punished for their "blasphemy." But then something literally knocked him off his horse. He met Jesus.

The conversation Jesus and Saul have is an interesting one. Jesus asks him, "Saul, Saul, why are you persecuting me?" Imagine what goes through Saul's mind at that point. He has been persecuting a lot of people. He watched as Stephen was stoned by the council. Yet the question is odd. How can Saul be expected to answer it? So he begs for more information: "Who are you, Lord?" Whoever the source of this voice is, he is no mere mortal. So Saul calls this cosmic stranger he has never met "Lord." It won't be the last time.

Finally Jesus introduces himself: "I am Jesus whom you are persecuting."

Of course Saul isn't too happy to hear this. He wasn't prepared for this answer. The last person he expected to have to address as "Lord" was Jesus. Furthermore, even with all the people he had been persecuting, Jesus was not one of them; Saul had never actually met Jesus.

So the conversation gets a bit one-sided at this point. Saul has nothing left to say; words and sensibility fail him. Jesus continues with some instructions for him, but I have a feeling they were repeated later, under conditions more conducive to comprehension. At this point Saul is taking in very little.

"I am Jesus whom you are persecuting." I think Saul/Paul spent many of his next few days and weeks thinking about that one. As a result of his meditations Paul came to a deep understanding of the nature of the church. From this experience Paul got his favorite image for the church: the body of Christ.

Jesus doesn't say, "I am Jesus whose friends you are persecuting," or "I am Jesus whose disciples you are persecuting," or "I am Jesus whose church you are persecuting." Rather, Jesus identifies so closely with his people that he equates himself with his followers corporately. In other words, when the church is persecuted, Christ feels the pain. The "body of Christ" image is not simply metaphor; it is reality, at a fundamental level. To be a member of the church is to be joined to Jesus. And vice versa: to have anything to do with Jesus requires participation in his body.

Jesus tells Saul why he has appeared to him. He is going to send Saul to the Gentiles. Saul's appointed task is to open people's eyes and to turn them from Satan to God, so that they will receive forgiveness . . . That's it, right?

No, receiving forgiveness from sins is not the ultimate destiny of those who respond to Paul's preaching, as important as that is. Rather, Jesus goes to all the trouble to call Paul in this dramatic way in order to accomplish a further goal: "so that they may receive forgiveness of sins *and a place among those who are sanctified by faith in me*" (v. 18).

For the Gentiles who will respond to Paul's preaching, and for us today, the process is not complete until people *take their place* within the body. Taking a place means more than finding a church to attend on Sunday mornings when nothing else is going on. It means more than finding a pew to sit in. It means entering the community of the people of God and taking up your role in God's plan for his people. It means being a functioning member of the body of Christ.

Several attitudinal barriers can make it difficult to find our places within the local body of believers. Each of these can keep us from satisfying involvement in church. No one will find a perfect church. If we have eyes to see all the things wrong with a church, we quickly will. That reaction can prevent us from receiving what God wants us to receive.

1. Consumer versus participant. The *consumer* attends a church service and rates it the way a reviewer might blurb a movie: "Two thumbs up!" "Very moving!" "A total snooze." The consumer is there to purchase a product, whether the product is strong biblical teaching or rockin' worship. The consumer pays for this product by the time he spends, and perhaps by giving to the weekly offering—fair (if nominal) payment for services rendered. The consumer reads the church bulletin looking for goods and services that might be interesting: a Bible study this week, a singles night next week, a monthly men's prayer breakfast. The consumer feels free to come to the service (or any activity of the church) late and to leave early whenever a prior engagement or other work interferes.

The *participant* views the church service or activity as much more than something just to enjoy or evaluate. The participant expects to contribute (and hence enjoys the experience much more). She contributes to the worship by her own singing, contributes to the church budget by her tithing and contributes to the warmth and friendliness of the church by her greetings to visitors after the service. The participant comes early and stays late, as there are always little ways to help prepare for the activity or to clean up afterward.

2. Attender versus member. The *attender* makes numerous decisions every week regarding the church: "Will I go to the 8:30 service today, or the 11:00, or not at all?" "Do I have time to make it to the young adults Bible study this evening?" "Do I really have time to stay for the monthly potluck? (If so I need to go buy some potato chips.)" All these decisions are evaluated against the list of other priorities the attender has. Most weeks she may well choose to go to church and go to Bible study—she may look to others like a very faithful member. But her mentality is one of an attender.

The *member* makes a commitment to join the life of the church in certain ways. This makes the member's life much simpler. Many fewer decisions need to be made every week. He will attend the same worship service, the same small group and the same activities every week, not because he has an uneventful or routine life but because membership in the community of the church is top priority for him. He organizes his work schedule around his church involvements, and other priorities fall in line after the commitments he has made to and with his church community.

The attender asks the question every week, every event: "Am I going?" The member asks different questions: "Whom can I bring with me? Whom can I invite to join me?" Since the member knows on Wednesday morning what he will be doing Thursday night, he can ask his friend at work, "Bill, would you be interested in joining me after work tomorrow for pizza and then a Bible study with some friends from my church?"

3. Critic versus partner. The *critic* keeps a mental scorecard of the church's strengths and weaknesses. He analyzes how people perform certain roles: how the worship was led, what songs were chosen, who prays and how well they did. He appreciates quality special music and is able to identify real talent when it is present *or absent.* The critic notices the friendliness of the greeters, the quality and abundance of the food offered during fellowship time and the confidence of the pianist. The critic discerns the wisdom, warmth and humor of the pastor. And certainly the critic evaluates the biblical depth and exegetical rigor of the sermon.

If you were to talk to the critic about his reflections, he would ask, "Why does *the church* do it this way?" "Why do *you guys* pray like this?" "Why do *they* sing these songs?" He may compare the church with his former group: "Back home *we* do Communion this way . . ." In each statement the critic makes it clear that he is on the outside of the church looking in, making critical evaluations (positively and negatively). He keeps himself standing apart from the people of God.

The *partner* also has a critical, evaluative capacity but uses it very differently. The partner, as an insider, wants the worship service, the small group experience, the service activity, even the fellowship time after worship to be the best it can be. The partner may have heard a new song she wants to introduce in worship, so she speaks with one of the worship leaders. Or she may be concerned that new people are not being welcomed effectively, so she talks with her small group about making a conscious effort to do so. Or she knows that the pianist is new and a little uncomfortable, so she makes it a point to affirm and encourage him after worship every week. Or, noticing the church's lack of interest in missions, she brings a concrete proposal to the church leadership or congregational meeting for discussion. While the critic says, "Why do *you guys* do it this way?" the partner says, "Would it be possible for *us* to do it like this?"

Paul's ministry was to open people's eyes, to call them to turn from Satan to God so that they might receive forgiveness *and* to take their place among those being sanctified by faith in Jesus. *Consumer, attender, critic:* these attitudes prevent people from taking their place in the body. They are the attitudes of clients of an institution rather than of fellow travelers on a journey. People who adopt these attitudes do so to protect themselves, their schedules and their prior commitments. They may do so out of fear of losing control of their lives, yet they lose out.

Participant, member, partner: adopting these postures toward the church makes taking a place that is satisfying and rewarding. These attitudes make us into fellow caravaners, people who have joined others on a journey toward the heavenly city. This approach makes it possible to experience true community in a church setting. Deeper friendships, greater spiritual growth, more profound understanding of Scripture, daily reliance on God—the door to all of these is opened when you take your place among those who are being perfected by God.

Openness to Church Renewal

I said in the first section of this chapter that God is at work renewing his universal church and many of his local churches. It is impossible for any of us through sheer effort and planning to bring renewal to a church—God must bring it through a fresh outpouring of his Spirit. But we can participate in God's renewing work in a church, if we welcome it and can see it coming.

"No one puts new wine into old wineskins; otherwise, the wine will burst the skins, and the wine is lost, and so are the skins; but one puts new wine into fresh wineskins" (Mark 2:22). Jesus tells this short parable in response to a question about his religious practices. His disciples weren't fasting regularly according to the fashion of the day. Challenged to justify their behavior, Jesus says that it wouldn't be appropriate for his disciples to fast "as long as they have the bridegroom with them." Fasting is supposed to help you focus your heart on God, but while Jesus is around the disciples have God in their midst. Fasting is not necessary at this time.

But then Jesus tells the parable of the wineskins, a commentary on the whole of the tension between Jesus and the Pharisees. In this episode and in the next two in Mark, the central issue is the conflict between the old and the new. The old is the Pharisees, the way they fast and the way they observe the sabbath. The new is Jesus and his approach to these same things. In the words of the parable, the Pharisees were trying to put the new wine of Jesus' presence and message into their old wineskins, their familiar and revered religious structures. Jesus says that to do that will destroy both the old and the new. Nothing of value will remain.

The parable makes a distinction between the wine and the wineskins. The new thing God is doing, its essence, is the wine. The structure that holds the new thing, the vehicle that conveys it, is the wineskin. This distinction is something that the Pharisees failed to see.[3]

For those of us familiar with the Gospels it is easy to forget that the Pharisees weren't always the bad guys. A century or so previous to Jesus' appearance in Palestine, the Pharisees were a radical reform movement within Judaism. After the return from the exile, this group wanted to keep Israel faithful to God so that God would once again look favorably on his chosen people. They expected the imminent return of the Messiah, who would restore Israel to its former glory. Their zeal for the sabbath, the law and religious observance was originally motivated by a desire to see God move with power among his people.

So at one point these structures (strict observance of the sabbath, rigid fasting practices) were themselves new wineskins into which God had poured his renewing Spirit. But by the time of Jesus' coming they were old and in need of replacement with fresh structures. Any attempt to force the new outpouring of God's Spirit into old structures was sure to result in destruction. In the death of Jesus we see the most graphic depiction of the destruction that results when the old and the new come into conflict.

This process has happened repeatedly throughout the history of the people of God and will continue to happen. The new structures into which God pours his Spirit become old as his people begin to trust in the structures rather than in him. The Pharisees took the Mosaic law, given by God to point his people to faith in him, and they began to trust in that law—its codification, objectification and proper execution—rather than in the God who gave it. They pursued the law, a law of faith, as if it were based on works (Romans 9:31-32).

This same process happens today when any church begins to rely on the structure rather than the Spirit who inhabits it. A few hundred years ago, singing English hymns rather than Latin chants was an innovation that brought greater fervor in worship. Yet those same hymns today, for many, can kill rather than release joy in worship. The monthly church potluck, while at one time a loving reenactment of the early church's fellowship meals, may in some churches have become a chore that only the most dutiful members are willing to endure. In each case meaningful worship and satisfying fellowship are God-inspired goals, but the particular structures used to achieve these goals will need to change over time. At any point a church may grow to trust in its structures of worship, fellowship, service, discipleship or leadership more than in the God who directs and shapes and energizes those structures through his Spirit. If this happens, then the church has undergone potentially deadly institutionalization. The church has ceased to be a caravan. It needs to experience renewal.

A church is like its individual members: imperfect, with strengths as well as weaknesses. We want to be able to see the church in the light of growth and renewal, just as we want to experience growth and renewal in our own lives. If we have become participants, members and partners in the churches of which we are a part, we will be given opportunities to participate in the renewing work of God among his people. God may give us eyes to identify some of the old wineskins in the church. With the commitment of a member we will be able to perceive weakness and need for change without impatience or revulsion. More than simply identifying the problem, we will find ourselves called to be part of the solution.

Elusive Community and Everyday Churches

Many Christians active in college fellowships have a difficult time joining churches after college. This is not necessarily simply because of poor motivation on the part of recent graduates. Below I offer the recent stories of several highly motivated graduates who experienced a bumpy transition into a variety of churches. Each entered his or her church with a participant-member-partner posture, but all found their investment in church disappointing. See if you identify with any of them.

Maya: My church involvement since graduation has been one of extremes. When I first came into contact with my church, I felt like I had come home and became a member immediately. The style of worship was similar to that of the churches I grew up in. As I stayed, though, it became increasingly difficult to put forth the energy to meet people. For a while I considered changing churches, after deciding that many people were not very interested in relationships. I had expended a lot of energy in the beginning to meet people and got about 5 percent of that back—it was very discouraging. I prayed and decided that I was going to stop expecting people to return my phone calls and initiative.

Kendall: While I learned a lot through my involvement with my church and respect it in many ways, discipleship and community are noticeably lacking there. I saw an endless group of people coming in without the base of partnership with which to minister to them.

Leslie: I've done most of the things organized churches do—social groups, service groups, outreach groups, study groups and leadership groups. I spent almost three years on a parish vestry. Most of my work in the church didn't help me or strengthen me to be more of a Christian in daily life—not directly, anyway. And it all took up incredible amounts of energy, leaving other areas of my life neglected for far too long.

Jan: I was involved in a Korean church as the youth pastor, but I couldn't foresee the lack of care I would receive in this environment as opposed to my college days. The church had no conscious ministry of caring for its leaders. In my case, I was expected to perform and supply the kids with teaching each week. But I was totally alone. This was a difficult, lonely and spiritually dry year.

Each of these people joined a church with the expectation of active participation, and they all jumped in. But each found church involvement disappointing (or worse) because of, in part, the failure of the church to offer satisfying community.

In many churches God is already bringing renewal in the experience of community. Yet many churches still have a long way to go. If you have enjoyed community in the college setting, you may eventually be able to participate with God in his renewing work in the church you join. But in the short term you must ask, "Where can I find the quality of community within the church context that I need to grow in my own faith?"

The previous chapter outlined a model for community with critical commonalities: common commitments, common vision and common life. These form the basis of any healthy community, Christian or otherwise. Ideally, your local church should offer community according to these principles. Yet as we have seen, the reality is often far different. Can you ensure an experience of community as you enter a church?

The most certain way of finding community in a new church is to bring it with you. Then at least you know it is there. That is the best chance you will have of experiencing community. I say this not because of a pessimistic view of churches but because of a realistic understanding of community: it takes work and a long time to form. So if you have community available, bring it with you.

How do you bring community to a church? The concept is simple: you start with community and then, as a community, you join a church. It involves calling together a group of people who have decided to be the caravan-type community of God's people, who have made a decision to follow God together after college. Each member of the group may need to subordinate some of his or her own tastes and preferences in order to find a church where the community is able to worship God and grow in love for one another and for others.

This is a strategy for planting a *seedling community*. This small group is not meant to be full-grown, fully developed shady-oak-tree community, but simply a seedling, already sprouted and prepared for growth. Your hope would be to invite others into your group, so that the sense of community can grow numerically as well as in depth. Over time your seedling community may become the shady-oak-tree type, fully rooted in the soil of the church.

I know of Christian households of four graduates where the members attend three different churches. Any potential for bringing the Christian community they could enjoy into their church is lost because their church commitments do not overlap.

I want to emphasize at this point that this recommendation doesn't imply that deep community is not available in most churches. My suspicion is that satisfying community is possible in more churches than one might expect, but that it will take work to discover and develop. But even in the best church with the most satisfying community, the experience of joining the church and its community will be smoother and faster if done by a group who themselves are a growing community.

At the same time I realize that this isn't always possible. You may not have access any longer to the community and partnerships you enjoyed while in college. The rest of this chapter offers some help and hope for you as well. A case-study approach will allow us to explore specific strategies for church involvement.

Church Involvement Case Study

What do you want in a church? What do you look for? On what criteria do you evaluate churches as good or bad, worth joining or not? These are fundamental questions for any Christian, but especially for people making the transition beyond college. Read the following descriptions of three churches, thinking as you read about what you might do to get involved in them.

University Baptist Church. UBC is a relatively young church, planted about ten years ago. Currently it has a regular attendance of about 125. Appropriately named, it is situated near a university, and about one-third of its attenders are undergraduates or graduate students. Many of the rest are young professionals and recent college grads. (It has few families with older children.) The worship style is contemporary, with some hymns. A variety of people are involved in the worship service, through leading worship, reading Scripture, sharing ministry highlights and making announcements. The sermons are Bible-based, relevant and challenging.

UBC is a church with vision to reach out in love and compassion to the poor in its neighborhood. It sponsors a clothes closet and food pantry, serving over 150 families per month. A few people have become Christians and have joined the church through this ministry. The closet/pantry also serves the church as a place to call new attenders to get more involved. Some of the closest relationships that have developed in the church have done so in the closet/pantry ministry. Many of the leaders of the church came into leadership through consistent involvement in this ministry.

UBC also places a priority on getting people into weekly small groups, and the pastors advertise them extensively during the fall of each year, when new groups are forming and old ones are changing membership or dividing. Perhaps 30 percent of the church body is in a church small group (many of the students are involved in on-campus Bible studies instead). The small groups vary in size, format and leadership; some of them foster deep relationships and a form of community while others have fizzled. A couple of these groups have offered some accountability to their members, but in the other small groups that has not been a goal. There is no development strategy for new group leaders or ongoing training for those who are in leadership already.

Vineyard Christian Fellowship. VCF is a charismatic church that has grown to 650 in attendance in the last ten years, although its growth rate has slowed in the past year. The worship service features a contemporary worship band with electronically amplified and mixed sound. The casual style of dress and seeker-friendly format make the service and the church as a whole very accessible for unchurched people who are visiting for the first time. The church desires to demonstrate the power of God and give people an experience of his presence. In this way the church ministers both to non-Christians as they turn to God as well as to Christians as they need healing and growth in their relationships with him. The Sunday-morning teaching is varied in quality but is focused on Scripture.

The main discipleship and community structure of the church is the kinship group, in which eight to fifteen people gather weekly for worship, prayer, sharing and teaching in a mix varying from group to group and week to week. Just over half of all the attenders are in a kinship group or ministry group, though commitment levels in the kinship groups vary widely. Some of the kinships focus on specific needs or populations. One kinship, for singles, actually includes a leadership training component, a second meeting per week for those who want training to lead inductive Bible studies and care for people in a kinship setting. Other kinships deal with adult survivors of sexual abuse, those in recovery from divorce and those in recovery from a homosexual lifestyle.

Ministry teams, such as the worship team, the outreach team and prayer teams, meet and become centers of relationship for those involved. For many these commitments serve the function of the kinship group as well as providing an avenue for ministry. Leadership in the church is functional and fluid, not hierarchical or fixed. The pastoral staff is open to new ideas and is willing to help people with new ideas make them happen. Lay ministry is heavily emphasized.

Trinity Episcopal. Trinity Episcopal Church is an older church in transition, operating with its second interim rector in two years. The worship style is liturgical, with singing of psalms and prayers, and includes some contemporary music and choruses. The congregation participates actively in worship, with hearty singing and congregational open prayer. The teaching is always based in Scripture, and the sermons are expected to impact daily life. The church has about 150 in worship, of whom about sixty are in "sharing groups"; most of these sixty are young professionals, single or married with no kids.

The weekly sharing groups include some Bible study, and accountability of some kind is at least a goal for them. Fellowship is an articulated goal and definite strength of these groups. The church has maintained several service ministries to children and the homeless, but these programs are in flux until the new rector is chosen. Leadership for the ministry groups is self-selected, and little strategic direction or training is given to leaders. The other main relational group is the choir—about thirty are involved. The choir population is something of a cross-section of the church by age and socioeconomic background.

Study your own church. The next section will look back at the three example churches and offer strategies for church involvement. But before you go ahead, take some time to think about the church you are in (or any church with which you are fairly familiar). To receive the most benefit from this exercise, consider the following questions before you look at the next section.

1. Assess the strengths and weaknesses of the church in light of the basic elements of community—accountability, partnership and fellowship (see chapter five).

2. How do people enter relationships in the church? What types of relationships do they have? (Factors: size of church, type and frequency of small group gatherings, geographical tightness of community.)

3. Who are the leaders? What does the leadership structure of the church look like? How do people become leaders? What are the criteria for leadership?

4. What opportunities are there to find people open to or eager for community and able to be real partners?

☐ teaching Sunday school
☐ small groups
☐ involvement in an adult Sunday-school class
☐ membership on a committee
☐ local outreach

Where would you find people with whom you could build partnership? What do you do to enter into partnership and friendship with them?

5. Keeping in mind the priorities discussed in this and the previous chapter, what would you do if you were going to attend this church

☐ alone, without anyone else you know?
☐ in partnership with one or two others from your campus?

For group reflection. If you are in a small group, you may want to come up with and discuss your own case study of church involvement. Have one person in your group describe a real church (home church, current or former church) with real strengths and weaknesses. The church doesn't have to be either a paragon of perfection or the very essence of death, but probably is best somewhere in between. People will then ask questions of the person familiar with the church and try to answer the questions given above. Obviously this kind of exercise can be even more useful if the entire small group attends the same church. Make real plans and commitments as you study your own church.

Strategies for Involvement

My hope is that you have given some thought to the questions in the last section and that you have familiarized yourself with the case-study churches I've described. Now let's turn to specific strategies for involvement, using the case studies as illustrations.

Look for a small group. Each of the three churches mentioned above has a small group structure. Kinship group, home fellowship, singles Bible study, sharing group—whatever the name, find a small group and join. Small groups vary even within the same church according to leadership styles and personalities, so it would be best to meet the leader(s) or key members even before you visit. If you enter a church with a "seedling community" (a few friends who share your vision), you all may want to join the same small group. If your "seedling" community has five or more people, plan to divide into a couple of small groups, rather than all joining a single group and inundating it. But at least try to join groups in pairs. In this way you can bring some of the relational strength you have with one another into the context of the small group, strengthening both your prior relationships and the quality of your new small group experience.

Get involved in relationship-building structures. If the church doesn't have a small group structure (though fewer and fewer churches don't), other structures may foster relationships in the church. Even if you *are* able to find a small group, participation in other activities as well may give you greater opportunity for relational breadth. For example, in the Episcopal church you could join the choir. In the Vineyard you might join one of the ministry teams. Some churches have new members classes or adult Sunday-school classes. These involvements may change over time, but investment early on will help you get to know more people and enter more quickly into the life of the community.

Take initiative in relationships. People may or may not take initiative with you—don't wait for them to make the first move, and don't judge the church by the standards of your student fellowship. Go ahead and invite people out for lunch after church. If you gear up for a period at the beginning during which you will take a great deal of initiative with people, you will find opportunities to develop growing friendships.

Join ministry that is already happening. Eventually you may have vision and ability to begin a new ministry within the church, but at the beginning it's more important to join what is already going on. This will help you understand the reasons behind the church's particular ministry emphasis; it will help you to be a better partner—not a critic—to the church. For example, UBC emphasizes involvement in the clothes closet and food pantry; get involved there. VCF uses ministry teams for worship, prayer and outreach; based on your gifts and interests, join one of these ministries. (Again, if you have friends entering the church with you, invite them to join you in one of these ministries.) The Episcopal church is undergoing transition—it may be that soon you will be able to contribute or implement your ideas as the church struggles to move forward in ministry.

Enter as a servant. Look for small, simple ways to help, to chip in: setting up chairs or helping to clean up after a meeting or meal, collecting the bulletins left in the pews, volunteering for nursery duty, assisting certain elderly or needy members with simple tasks. The best thing you have to offer at first is simply your availability.

Consider ministry to the least of all. Often churches have a difficult time finding enough teachers and helpers for children's Sunday school. Consider becoming a helper among the children. I know of no greater way to enter a church with a humble servant attitude. Don't jump in as the teacher; be the helper, whose main job is helping the children glue the face on a paper plate. The adults who are already giving their lives to these children have learned something fundamental about the gospel. Don't shoot for the elder board; shoot for working alongside the people who love children. Learn from the teachers and the children in that setting. To such as these belongs the kingdom of God (Mark 10:14).

Don't enter leadership quickly. Any church in which leadership is an opportunity for healthy spiritual growth will not put people into leadership too quickly. If the church is desperate for leadership you must ask why—probably leaders are not being developed, trained or supported. Even if you have led small groups before, you will probably want to experience one in the church setting before you take on small group leadership. Your willingness to come in on the ground level will disarm those who might otherwise have resented you, and eventually you will gain greater freedom to lead and innovate.

Don't hop around. Stay in one small group and in one area of ministry for a while trying to develop partners. Jesus told his disciples, when they were visiting towns two by two, to stay in the first house that received them until they left the town (Mark 6:10). The priority is to build partners and deep relationships, the foundation of community. Your first friends and partners in ministry in a church may remain so even if your interests and ministry focus eventually change.

Pray for your church. As you pray, God will give you a soft heart toward the quirks and problems of your church. He will make you into a participant-member-partner and will give you his eyes for the church. God may direct you to people who need encouragement. And he will show you how much you have to learn from the wisdom and maturity of the leaders.

Be patient and expect God to work. Be patient with yourself—you are building the foundation for a lifetime of church involvement. Be patient with other people—they may not share all of your convictions, yet God may be very much at work in them. You may have more to learn than you think. And be patient with the church. God is more committed to this church than you are. If God intends to renew the church, one good sign of that is that he is raising up people to pray for the church. If you aren't praying, then don't be judging.

Keep your youth in proper perspective. Expect to learn, and be open about your need for growth and development. Enter the church as a learner, not an expert. Ask yourself, "What are the things this church has that I need?" Acknowledge to yourself and others that you are new at postcollege life and that you are still in transition.

Look for people from whom you can learn. You may find an older man or woman in the church who exudes love for God. This person may be booked up with activities and involvements and initially may not have much time to meet personally with you. But perhaps you could join one of his or her ministry committees or small groups. This may give you opportunity to develop a relationship that could prove fruitful for your own discipleship over time. The same could be said for peer relationships and potential partnerships. When you identify people you think you could learn from and enjoy, take steps to build relationships with them. Expect that your church will have people you can learn from, and it probably will.

Be prepared to learn from many different people. In college we are exposed to a relatively narrow spectrum of people from whom we are expected to learn: professors and students (we *aren't* expected to learn from janitors and lunch-line servers). That's why we need to open our minds: many of the people we meet in church may possess less formal education than we do but much more wisdom. If we met these people on the campus we might be tempted to ignore them, but in the church they are our brothers and sisters—our *older* brothers and sisters. If we carry any educational elitism into church, we are likely to resist or dismiss the leadership and insights of men and women who have been gifted by God.

Criteria for Evaluation

The fact that God is at work in a particular church doesn't necessarily imply that you should join it. Many factors contribute to preferences in church selection; debating preferential factors would be like saying, "You should eat only chocolate-chip ice cream."

But some aspects of a church are not like eating chocolate-chip ice cream—they are more like bread and butter or meat and potatoes (or for some people, sprouts and tofu). They are essential for a healthy diet, not simply dessert after the meal. If you are not certain about the church you plan to join, you may find it helpful to reflect on the following questions.

Where can I find community? Much of this chapter has focused on finding satisfying community in the context of the church. Yet in some churches this may not be possible. Do community-forming structures exist? Church small group structures vary, but most of them at least offer the hope (and desire) for community. Obviously small groups that meet only once per month or every other Sunday evening for one hour will not be conducive to the kind of community you are hoping to find in a church. This may be a good indicator that the church doesn't really value community.

Where is Scripture being studied? Some degree of happy fellowship may exist in a church without a true sense of common convictions and common commitments. Community itself is based on a corporate life with God, including both prayer and Scripture study. If there is no place in the church where Scripture is being studied in a way that can be transformative, then you will want either to start such a study (if you plan to commit yourself there) or else to move. Corporate Scripture study may look different from what it looked like in college. Sermons on Sunday morning may be a part of the corporate Scripture study of the church, but hopefully not the whole thing. Are people willing to spend time to study the Bible? Is the Bible authoritative in people's lives?

Many churches would like to have Bible study in small groups, in Sunday-school classes or at other times. Church leaders are not usually resistant to the idea of Scripture study, but some have little idea about how to make it practical and accessible. Often the limiting factors are time and desire—people don't value Bible study enough to set aside the time. If you desire to introduce your church to transformative Scripture study, then start small and invite people who will be willing to give the time it takes to do it right. Over time this will win a hearing among others, as people share about the experience they have.

Ultimately, if there is no hope for common Scripture study in the church you are considering, then what shapes that church is simply the opinions of its members. If the church is not listening to God through his Word as a body, it would be better to keep looking for a church that is.

Can I invite my friends to worship here? It is critical to attend a church where you feel comfortable inviting other people, including non-Christian friends from work (or your chosen ministry arena, if it is not within the church). Different factors come into play. For example, *you* may be willing to drive forty minutes to attend a church with a happening worship service. But will it be possible for you to drag your work friends all that distance? Would a more geographically accessible church make a significant difference? Very probably.

Other factors include the style and length of the worship service and the ethnic composition of the church. If you are living in an urban neighborhood with the intention of doing ministry there, it's crucial to attend a church in which friends and people from the neighborhood would feel welcome and at home. That may mean choosing a bilingual church if your ministry is to nonnative English speakers. That may mean that the style of worship of the service doesn't quite match your preferred style—that you are less at home there so that your friends can be more at home. That may mean that you as a Korean-American choose not to join a Korean church if your friends at work are mostly Caucasian.

In other words, the vision of the church should roughly overlap or relate to your own vision for ministry. If your vision is for student ministry, your church should be attractive to students. If you minister to the homeless, the church should be a place you feel comfortable bringing them to. Ask yourself, "Is the church attractive and open to the people I would want to bring?"

Will this church help me grow as a Christian? The church should be challenging to your own spiritual growth. Many churches are better at getting people to do things than at helping them to grow spiritually. Many are better at using leaders than developing them. You may have learned how to lead a Bible study through the training program of your college fellowship. Many churches don't have such a training program; their trained leaders all come from other fellowships and churches.

Pray to see this church with God's eyes. Ask yourself, "What are the strengths and emphases of this church that I see lived out in the character and choices of its core members?" If your list is a short one, then perhaps you should look for another church.

What is this church's doctrinal statement? Are there any doctrinal peculiarities? It is beyond the scope of this book to describe or prescribe a certain set of doctrines to look for, beyond the basics of belief in Jesus Christ as God incarnate and a reliance on Scripture as the Word of God. Every church thinks that its doctrines are the best or truest summary of God's revelation to humankind. However, one warning sign is a church or group that essentially teaches that every other church is apostate and that to be saved people must be members of this particular church body or denomination. Often this will come out of a peculiar focus on an aspect of the Christian life or a weighted emphasis on obscure passages in Scripture. An emphasis on the right baptism or the right sacramental meal, an addition to the historical "salvation by faith alone" formula or a focus on the teaching of some recent "prophet" or additional "scriptures"—any of these things can take a church out of the mainstream of historical Christianity and into cult status.

If your previous growth as a Christian is not valued in the church you have begun attending, that is a good indication that this church sees itself as the only true church. Look instead for a church that has a humble recognition that it isn't the only group of people trying to follow God faithfully, is open to new understanding as God pours out his Spirit in new ways, yet meanwhile is still committed to its doctrines and practices.

Is the church open to God's agenda for renewal? A church that is open to renewal sees the structures as servants of the people of God and not the other way around. Openness doesn't mean that people lack strong orthodox convictions—biblical renewal doesn't involve inventing new beliefs about God. Openness to renewal is openness to new structures, new ways of achieving time-honored goals.

As you see the need for renewal in your own life and the life of the church, ask yourself, "Do the leaders seem open to moving in new directions?" Even if these new structures, small groups or worship elements aren't the ones you might have chosen, if the church is open to change at this level that is a good sign. If the church hasn't changed its format or its ministry and care structures in twenty years, and no change is on the horizon, this is a sign of rigid institutionalization. Go to a church where the hand of God is more visible in shaping his people.

* * *

The problem in joining any church is a little bit like Groucho Marx's problem in joining a club. He once said, "I wouldn't want to join any club that would have me as a member." We all want to find the perfect church, yet the reality is that if we found it and joined it we would ruin it.

Churches are often like the Dream Team, with each of us embarrassed by the actions of fellow team members. Perhaps with clearer vision we would see that our brothers and sisters in Christ are often embarrassed by us as well. So we must do the best we can—and we have no choice but to find a church where we can band together as we extend and receive God's grace through his people gathered in his name.

■ *For Reflection*
Models of the Church
☐ How have you viewed your church as a commissary, dispensing

goods and services as you have need of them?

☐ By what aspects of your church have you tended to evaluate it (its community life, its performance of certain functions, its ability to meet your needs)?

Take Your Place in the Body

Consider the three contrasts: consumer-participant, attender-member, critic-partner. Obviously these pairs form continuums. Most of us probably fall somewhere in the middle.

☐ Think about the church community of which you are a part. How would you rate yourself on each scale? Perhaps you could make a list of things you do or think that are characteristic of each of the attitudes contrasted.

☐ What would it mean for you to move more to the participant-member-partner side of the charts?

Openness to Church Renewal

☐ Have you grown to rely on some structures of God's grace instead of God in your college fellowship or in your current church?

☐ Is it possible to imagine God's grace administered to you through other structures?

☐ How can you be an agent of renewal in your current church or community?

For Further Reading

Eller, Vernard. *The Outward Bound.* Grand Rapids. Mich.: Eerdmans, 1980.

Hauerwas, Stanley, and William Willimon. *Resident Aliens.* Nashville: Abingdon, 1989.

Petersen, Jim. *Church Without Walls.* Colorado Springs: NavPress, 1992.

Snyder, Howard A. *Liberating the Church.* Downers Grove, Ill.: Inter-Varsity Press, 1983.

7
A Mobilized Lifestyle for the Kingdom

Glenn and Matt live together in a studio apartment in the Tenderloin district, one of the most economically depressed areas of San Francisco. They live in a five-floor building that has seventy studio apartments, most housing families of five or more. The population of the building is predominantly recent immigrants from Southeast Asia.

Glenn and Matt had a vision to begin a tutoring program for the kids living there. When they moved into the building, they made a radical decision. Instead of each moving into a single studio, they both moved into one studio. They rented an adjoining studio apartment as a study center, opening it up as a drop-in library, lounge and hangout for the kids in the building and the neighborhood. Each of them staffs the study center one night a week, and others from their church join the rotation. Glenn and Matt are teachers at the local Galileo High School and see many of the kids from the neighborhood in class. At school they have become friends with a number of the teenage boys, and about a year ago they began a Bible study on Friday nights for these guys. Recently four of them became Christians, and eight or ten others have joined the study.

Glenn and Matt are not alone in their vision to incarnate the love of God in this place. Paula and Sandy, also recent college graduates, live in another studio apartment in the same building. They attend the same church and are also involved in tutoring kids in the building at the study center. Paula recently left her former job to work for the local Family Literacy Program. She teaches English and helps immigrant families learn about the resources available to them. Paula herself is a Chinese immigrant via Vietnam; she speaks Cantonese and can empathize with the people with whom she works.

Glenn, Matt, Paula and Sandy have made choices about their lifestyles which are allowing them to have radical impact on people in need. Throughout this chapter we will examine how our lifestyles can be mobilized for the kingdom of God. We will look more closely at the choices and decisions these four people have made.

A Definition of Lifestyle

Lifestyle is an amorphous word, the heading for our lives' *miscellaneous* category. Questions of lifestyle include the following:

☐ What do you spend your money on?

☐ How do you spend your time?

☐ At what pace do you live?

☐ Where and how much do you eat?

☐ Where do you live?

☐ What spiritual disciplines do you practice?

☐ What do your vacations look like?

☐ What do you do with your leisure time?

Let me offer a simple definition of lifestyle that brings these diverse elements together:

Lifestyle:
the outworking of our values in our lives.

Do you agree? When confronted with this definition, I want to claim that my lifestyle may include things that don't really reflect my values.

But if I take a hard look at them, I would have to agree that they do reflect my values. For example, I used to eat fast food perhaps four times per week. That says something about the relative values I placed on nutrition, time and money. I may claim to value healthful living, but if I fail to eat healthfully or cannot ever seem to allocate time to fitness disciplines, then I must admit that I don't truly value what I claim to value.

Our lifestyles don't lie. They accurately reflect the value we give to competing interests and priorities. We cannot ignore people and claim to value them; we cannot disregard God and claim to honor him.

Jesus' Style

A young man walked up to Jesus one day as he was teaching in the temple. "Teacher," he said, "what is the greatest commandment?"

Jesus scanned the man's face. He listened intently to the man's tone. After a day of trick questions aimed at trapping him, it sounded as if this questioner was refreshingly sincere. Jesus was pleased to respond to a humble, uncontrived question. "The first is, 'Hear, O Israel: The Lord our God, the Lord is one; you shall love the Lord with all your heart, and with all your soul, and with all your mind, and with all your strength.' " Then Jesus added, "The second is this, 'You shall love your neighbor as yourself.' There is no other commandment greater than these" (Mark 12:28-31).

All of Jesus' teaching can be summarized by these two commandments, reduced simply to "Love God and love your neighbor." All of Jesus' calls for obedience, all of his ethical teachings, all of his parables, imperatives, rhetorical questions—everything Jesus said can be summarized by these simple (though not easy) commandments.

To Jesus, relationships were everything. Obviously simply knowing the commandments does not mean that obeying them is easy. So Jesus lived and taught, modeled and articulated what it means to love God and love people. Jesus' relationship with his Father displayed the nature of a true child's love relationship with the Father God. Jesus' servanthood to others illustrated what neighbor love is all about. Jesus' followers became disciples as they apprehended his model and teaching.

Jesus called his disciples to live by two priorities only: to love God and to love people. If we are to follow his teaching and example, these values should have *the shaping impact* on our lifestyles. Yet too often our lives reflect a multitude of other competing values at war within us; we make attempts to live consistently, but obstacles appear that undo our best efforts.

God, Work, Community, Church and Lifestyle

The diagram below illustrates how topics of the past four chapters and the topic of lifestyle fit together. The first set of circles graphically illustrate Fred's scattered life. Fred wants to have a place for God in his world, but God is not at the center of his life. God has a lot to do with church, has some overlap in his community and is factored into his lifestyle. But God is not at the center of any of these things. Fred's community includes some of his church world but also his work world, and these two worlds don't intersect at all. Fred's lifestyle is more influenced by his non-Christian friends and his work than by his Christian community or church. Fred's work has nothing to do with God. He certainly doesn't see himself as striving for the kingdom of God as he heads off to work each morning.

Compare this with the depiction of Susie's life. Susie has, at the

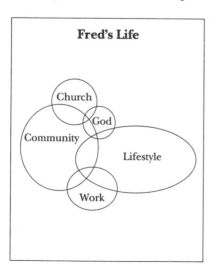

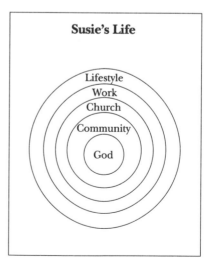

center and focus of her life, her relationship with God. She gives priority to her time in prayer and Scripture study, and it affects all she does. God is at the center of her closest friendships with other Christians. This deep community is found in her church and is central to her involvement there. Her "work"—that is, striving for the kingdom—includes her involvement in the church but goes beyond it to encompass her ministry and job outside the church. Finally, her lifestyle is centered on her active working for the kingdom, so that her time, money and value choices reflect her priorities of loving God and loving people.

The five circles can be understood as follows:

☐ The inner circle, relationship with God, is the heart of discipleship. If God is at the center, then we have rejected the world's lies regarding how life is to be lived and joy is to be found. The worship of God alone is the foundation of true joy and contentment.

☐ Community is our most vital human resource. It is the core of a satisfying experience in a church but also of a connected and satisfying life in the world.

☐ Church includes our core community as well as other relationships with and ministry to Christians in the local congregation.

☐ Work includes ministry in the church setting but also ministry in a secular environment and tentmaking. It involves all the ways we actively strive for God's kingdom.

☐ Lifestyle goes beyond active striving to the implicit choices we make and practical ways we mobilize our resources for our work, church, community and relationship with God.

Just a word about the diagrams. What is significant about the circles is what they include or exclude, not their size. The God circle in Susie's diagram is the smallest, but that doesn't mean it is least important. It is the center of each of the other circles, and hence it is the focus of her life as depicted here.

Susie is a fictitious character, but Glenn, introduced at the beginning of the chapter, is quite real. How does the set of circles work in his life? Having graduated from college with a degree in engineering, Glenn moved to San Francisco with some college friends. He became involved in a church right away and began looking for an opportunity for ministry. Meanwhile he was commuting two to three hours every day by train to his work in Silicon Valley. As Glenn joined a local ministry, he began to see himself as a missionary to the city. But his multifocused life was becoming frustrating. So Glenn, with his friend Matt, made several key decisions:

☐ Glenn and Matt decided to move into the Tenderloin area, where they had already begun to get involved in ministry.

☐ They switched to a church that had ministry involvement in their neighborhood and was very supportive of their efforts. There they met Paula and Sandy, and the four of them became the core of a community of people praying for and ministering in the Tenderloin.

☐ Glenn decided to earn a teaching credential. Afterward he found a teaching job at the local high school, where Matt had been teaching for a couple of years. Though Glenn had enjoyed his work as an engineer, he found that his sense of purpose required more focus than the commute and the work would allow. Since he began teaching, Glenn has spent a summer back at his engineering firm as a consultant. He enjoyed the short-term assignment but was glad to return to teaching in the fall.

Glenn was unsatisfied with a life that looked something like Fred's, described above. So Glenn made conscious choices to bring his life into focus, centered on his relationship with God and his sense of God's call on his life. Now his lifestyle supports his work, which is centered in his church and the core community living in and involved with the Tenderloin.

It is possible to choose *not* to live a scattered, distracted, undirected life. Each of us can begin to make choices that bring our lives into focus around the things that matter most.

The Centered Life

Jesus speaks about the impossibility of living a consistent life that has more than one center. He uses three images to make the same point:

Do not store up for yourselves treasures on earth, where moth and rust consume and where thieves break in and steal; but store up for yourselves treasures in heaven, where neither moth nor rust consumes and where thieves do not break in and steal. For where your treasure is, there your heart will be also.

The eye is the lamp of the body. So, if your eye is healthy, your whole body will be full of light; but if your eye is unhealthy, your whole body will be full of darkness. If then the light in you is darkness, how great is the darkness!

No one can serve two masters; for a slave will either hate the one and love the other, or be devoted to the one and despise the other. You cannot serve God and wealth. (Matthew 6:19-24)

Jesus says that the things you most value will be at the center of your life. You cannot live in the light of God if your focus is on other things. You cannot serve God and any other master. Jesus says that the unfocused life is an impossible one—your focus will return, but usually on something other than God. Jesus calls us to live our lives focused on, devoted to, fixed on God. It is no surprise that at this point in his teaching Jesus continues with a call to strive for the kingdom of God (Matthew 6:25-34).

Paul speaks of his single-focused life with the metaphor of the runner who is running a race in order to win the prize:

I have become all things to all people, that I might by all means save some. I do it all for the sake of the gospel, so that I may share in its blessings. Do you not know that in a race the runners all compete, but only one receives the prize? Run in such a way that you may win it. Athletes exercise self-control in all things; they do it to receive a perishable wreath, but we an imperishable one. So I do not run aimlessly, nor do I box as though beating the air; but I punish my body and enslave it, so that after proclaiming to others I myself should not be disqualified. (1 Corinthians 9:22-27)

But this one thing I do: forgetting what lies behind and straining forward to what lies ahead, I press on toward the goal for the prize of the heavenly call of God in Christ Jesus. Let those of us then who are mature be of the same mind; and if you think differently about anything, this too God will reveal to you. (Philippians 3:13-15)

The athlete is an apt image of someone whose entire lifestyle reflects his or her values and priorities. Serious athletes in training will spend most of their day mentally fixed on their goal. What they eat, when they sleep and how they spend their time—everything they do relates to and supports their overall objective. Paul is saying that he has this same kind of focus. He can say that he does *one thing*, that all his activity can be summarized as a pressing toward the finish line in his life and faith. And in both of these passages Paul calls his readers to think of life in the same way.

God's Economy and Our Resources

One day Jesus told a particularly shocking tale of graft and corruption in which the bad guy turns out to be a model for Christians!

> There was a rich man who had a manager, and charges were brought to him that this man was squandering his property. So he summoned him and said to him, "What is this that I hear about you? Give me an accounting of your management, because you cannot be my manager any longer." Then the manager said to himself, "What will I do, now that my master is taking the position away from me? I am not strong enough to dig, and I am ashamed to beg. I have decided what to do so that, when I am dismissed as manager, people may welcome me into their homes." So, summoning his master's debtors one by one, he asked the first, "How much do you owe my master?" He answered, "A hundred jugs of olive oil." He said to him, "Take your bill, sit down quickly, and make it fifty." Then he asked another, "And how much do you owe?" He replied, "A hundred containers of wheat." He said to him, "Take your bill and make it eighty." And his master commended the dishonest manager because he had acted shrewdly; for the children of this age are more shrewd in dealing with their own generation than are the children of light. And I tell you, make friends for yourselves by means of dishonest wealth so that when it is gone, they may welcome you into the eternal homes. (Luke 16:1-9)

How do we understand this parable? What was Jesus thinking?

The manager, or steward, in this parable could be compared to an accountant and investment manager combined. This steward was accused of wasting his master's goods, through either faulty accounting or poor decision-making. He was fired and told to turn over the accounts, the written records of business transactions. It is as if he were given two days' notice and told, "Have the records up to date and be ready to turn the books over to me at that time."

So he decided to fudge the books before turning them over to his master. He made friends essentially by giving away his master's money. By decreasing the amounts of debt people owed, he was making his master poorer and his master's clients wealthier. He hoped he could later turn these transactions into contacts and friendships he could "take to the bank." His plan was that these clients would be indebted to him and would welcome him into their homes when he was turned out.

The confusing part of this parable comes in verse 8, where the master discovered the dishonest steward's plan. Contrary to what we expect, the master commends the steward on his shrewdness. Why? Why wasn't the master angry with this steward who was giving away his goods?

Consider the personality of the master. This is a wealthy merchant, used to buying low and selling high, making money every time. The master is a shrewd businessman himself. He had fired the steward because the guy was wasting his money. Essentially he had fired the steward because he was *not* shrewd in his dealings. So in a moment of desperation, this inept steward has developed a plan that is *uncharacteristically shrewd*. When the master discovers the plan, he no doubt is not happy about it, but his own appreciation for shrewd thinking makes him commend his former steward for a sudden, unexpected display of shrewdness.

Here the parable ends and Jesus speaks to his listeners: "The children of this age are more shrewd in dealing with their own generation than are the children of light." To retranslate, "Worldly businessmen know how to use money to make friends, but Christians don't." Then Jesus goes on to say perhaps the most confusing thing of all: "And I tell you, make friends for yourselves by means of dishonest wealth so that when it is gone, they may welcome you into the eternal homes."

First let's consider what Jesus means by a few of these phrases. "Dishonest wealth" could be translated simply as "worldly wealth." Jesus is not speaking about wealth gained illegally. A few verses later, in Luke 16:11, Jesus contrasts worldly wealth with true riches, treasure in heaven. Second, Jesus speaks of "when it [worldly wealth] fails." Worldly money fails when life itself is over, when only true riches or treasure in heaven matters. It is not a question of "*if* it fails," since for all people money fails at the point of death. Finally, Jesus speaks of "the eternal homes." Here he is referring to heaven, where his disciples will live eternally with him and with one another.

So what is Jesus trying to tell his disciples? Jesus urges them to use money to make friends who will welcome them into heaven. Is Jesus telling people to buy friends?

The steward understands something about the resources he has available to him. First of all, *he knows that his wealth isn't his*. He has access to large amounts of wealth that he can give away at no cost to himself because it isn't his to begin with. Second, *he understands that he will not have access to this wealth for very long*. He wants to invest these fleeting resources in something that will last far beyond his access to them. He invests in relationships, in friendship with his master's clients.

The situation of this steward is our situation as well. Since we are disciples of our Lord Jesus, and created beings owned by God, none of our money, wealth or possessions are really ours. Our possessions and "the cattle on a thousand hills" (Psalm 50:10) are all God's. We are simply stewards of God's resources. So we can give them away at no cost to ourselves—they weren't ours in the first place! And like the steward in the parable, we have access to these resources for only a little time. Money will fail; life itself will fail.

If we understood what the steward understood, we too would be investing God's resources, on short-term loan to us, in eternal enterprises, in projects that will develop eternal wealth, treasure in heaven. On this earth the only eternal things around us are people. Cars, houses, boats, even companies and governments—none are eternal. They will all one day come to an end. Jesus told his disciples to invest their temporary, worldly wealth in other people who would become friends and welcome them into the dwelling places of heaven.

How does this happen? How do we make friends who will welcome us into heaven? By spending our resources so that people will come to know our generous and wealthy God. As we spend our money on people, we communicate that they are valuable. The gospel says that God so loved people that he spent his only begotten Son on the cross to save them. God used his resources to make friends who would celebrate with him in heaven. Jesus, in this parable, is telling us to do the same.

Jesus contrasts Christians ("children of light") to merchants like the master. Merchants of any era know all about making friends with money. Money is the way palms are greased, deals are made, government officials are satisfied. Money makes friends. But in the world, money is not simply a means, it is *the* end of all activity. In fact, people are too often simply a means to the end of making more money.

Jesus turns that relationship around. Money is not permanent; it is temporary and will fail. One way or the other, people are eternal beings; people are an end in themselves. Worldly merchants *use people* to *love money*. Money is their goal and their idol. Disciples of Jesus instead *use money* to *love people*. Serving people and bringing them into the kingdom is the goal. This is the greater joy by far: loving people into the kingdom, in part through the use of money. Disciples love what is worthy of love and use what is only meant to be used.

Albert Einstein made most of his discoveries through "thought experiments." A thought experiment is an experiment that is carried

	Worldly businessmen	Disciples of Jesus
Shrewdness:	Duplicity, cunning	Generosity
Goal:	Gain money	Love people
Tool:	People	Money
Motto:	"Use people to gain money"	"Use money to love people"

out only in the mind but that yields helpful insights. Consider this thought experiment: Suppose we were to pool all of our money in one bank account. Anyone who needed anything could have access to it at any time, and all income would be deposited jointly. And suppose we decided that this decision was irreversible. How would this change your own spending and saving patterns? What would be easy to spend money on? What purchases would be more difficult?

It would be much easier to spend money on one another, and it would be easier to be generous to those outside the community to whom we want to be a servant or a witness. Members of the group might move into shared housing, decreasing the monthly housing expense for the group. People would choose to share things, rather than each person having to own his or her own appliances, games, tools and luxuries. The most difficult purchases would involve personal spending on selfish wants beyond simple needs. Every dollar I spent on myself would mean a dollar less for the community and its ministry to others.

Now you might think this kind of community would become a grim place. Not so! Instead of sneaking off to buy myself some ice cream when I am down, I would have others who are looking to my interests and are aware of my discouragement. And since all of us would be eager to share the abundant resources of the community with those who are outside, "making friends for ourselves by means of worldly wealth," people on the fringes of our community would take great interest in what we are up to. The power of this approach to life would draw people in.

I began this discussion considering a simple thought experiment. Yet reflecting on Luke 16 helps us see that the hypothetical situation is, in important ways, reflective of reality. We are simply stewards of God's resources. As we begin to see our resources as God's, on loan for us to use *wisely* (though not stingily), it becomes easier to spend God's money on others. It becomes more difficult to spend money on myself, because God will hold me, his steward, accountable for the decision. It becomes a privilege and a joy to handle God's resources in this manner.

This mindset creates a new economy, God's economy. For example, when I buy ice cream for myself, nothing very eternal happens—if you don't count weight gain. But when I share God's resources with others in God's name, they are served genuinely and in a way that brings glory to God, the true provider. I benefit as well, as I receive the joy Jesus wants for his disciples as I too become a lover of people, not money or things (or ice cream). This then is God's economy: as we serve people with our money, they are brought into relationship with God. God, the engine of this economy, is glorified. We receive joy as we experience community with God's people and deep dependence on God.

Generosity

Viewing our resources the way the steward did in Luke 16 will have a liberating effect on our lifestyle: it frees us to be as generous with others as God has been with us. Yet during the transition beyond college it can be very tempting to have a tight hold on our money. Most of us are making the transition from net spenders (college tuition, room and board) to net producers (wages or salary). We are tempted to think that it will just take a few years to get on our feet financially, and *then* we can become very generous—or at least begin tithing. Yet *now* is the time to allocate resources toward our stated values. Don't wait for the distant future to begin to set the pattern of using money to love people.

Consider setting aside money in your budget for generosity. You may want to set aside 10 percent (a tithe) for giving to your church and supported ministry and then a second 10 percent for special needs and spontaneous generosity. If you will be earning $1,500 or more per month, it would be exciting to have $150 every month just to spend on people! As you are in ministry you may meet people whose needs God is intending to meet through your faithful generosity. God may intend to use you to minister to them on multiple levels, both physically and relationally. If you set money aside as you earn it, before long you will find plenty of creative ways to give it away or spend it wisely on people.

Generosity in community is contagious. One year I lived virtually rent-free because of the generosity of a friend. I was able to set aside what I would have paid in rent, about $200 a month, to give away. Because I received the generosity of another, I was able to be generous in turn. And as I live this way, it makes it easier for others to do so as well.

One form of generosity I have both received and given is to share rent in a household according to income and ability rather than according to the size of the bedroom. While at one time I lived rent-free, at another time I paid nearly twice as much rent as another person in my household because of the difference in our incomes, though in fact we shared the same bedroom. My generosity enabled Brian to participate more fully in ministry. My resources were part of the way God was providing for my friend while he too sought first the kingdom of God.

Hospitality

The importance of a lifestyle of hospitality is obscured because of the domestic "Good Housekeeping" images the term *hospitality* conjures up: an aproned 1950s mom taking a steaming apple pie out of the oven, or a table set for a fancy tea complete with dainty napkins, scones and an assortment of jams and preserves. But this does not cover the scope of the biblical notion of hospitality. In 1 Timothy 3:2 Paul says that a bishop or overseer must be, among other things, hospitable. What is hospitality that it would rank as a qualification for holding the highest church position mentioned in Scripture?

Let me define hospitality in a way that will make sense of its importance:

> *Hospitality:*
> *the ability to make a welcoming space for relationships to grow.*

The gospel is a relational gospel; those who foster growing relationships provide a fundamental ministry. Though Jesus had no home, he was hospitable—he gathered people together and drew them not simply to himself but also into relationship with one another. Hospitality is the ability to *make space*. Relationships need different kinds of space to be able to flourish.

Hospitality may involve many things:

☐ *Physical space*—a clean, neat living room, dining room or kitchen; a guest room, game room, TV room. Even a small apartment can be a warm place for people to gather, or it can be a disaster area no one enters without a hard hat.

☐ *Time*—setting aside time to encourage relationships to form. Inviting people over, visiting people, planning trips around seeing people.

☐ *Social space*—thinking about what would help people be at ease as they are forming new relationships: snacks, games and the like.

☐ *Emotional space*—asking questions in group settings that open people up or take the discussion to a deeper level. This also includes knowing which questions are appropriate and which may feel forced.

☐ *Spiritual space*—spending time in prayer and reflection to discern deeper needs in people, helping them enter more fully into relationships with others.

If you seriously want to mobilize your resources for the kingdom, begin to see things you already have as tools for hospitality, rather than as possessions that own you. For example, a house or apartment may be a wonderful kingdom asset, but it all depends on the attitudes and priorities of those who live there.

Hospitality requires that resources be set aside for it. You may have the most hospitable house imaginable, but if you have no time to invest in relationships, nothing will happen. The next section will examine simplicity as a means to mobilizing our resources for the kingdom. Yet you may decide to buy some expensive things in order to strive for the kingdom through hospitality. A TV with a VCR seems like a necessity in the materialistic acquisition race of our culture. Purchasing one thoughtlessly or selfishly would involve participation in that form of idolatry. Still, your household may decide that you want to be able to entertain others and provide a gathering place where relationships can form. For groups, a video night is far less expensive than a theater movie. For this economy of hospitality, as a group you might decide to purchase a VCR.

Taking another look at Glenn and Matt, we see the high value they placed on hospitality. Each could have afforded to rent a studio apartment for himself, and no one would have faulted them for extravagance. Or they could simply have chosen to share an apartment, and people would have marveled at their frugality. But instead they chose to double up in one apartment and rent a second so that they could have space for a study center and drop-in lounge. They set aside physical space so that relationships could grow. And they have seen much fruit. Kids, used to the cramped quarters of their family apartments, love to come by, whether for English tutoring or other academic help or simply to enjoy some attention and a safe place to relax. The extra rent Matt and Glenn pay each month is small compared to the study center's value to the kids. Glenn and Matt are using their worldly wealth to make friends for the kingdom of God.

Simplicity

The word *simplicity* summarizes the kind of lifestyle we are to be pursuing as disciples of Jesus Christ. If our lives are centered on God alone, we will live simply. If our sole pursuit is the kingdom of God, our priorities and values and the lifestyle choices that reflect them become simplified. In *Celebration of Discipline* Richard Foster says this is the foundation of simplicity: "Simplicity begins in inward focus and unity."[1] In the diagrams earlier in this chapter, simplicity is depicted in Susie's concentric circles. Each expanding circle of concern is centered on the inner and more fundamental circle, until our entire lifestyle is built around God and our desire to strive for his kingdom above all else.

On the other hand, if our lives have multiple centers, the resulting complexity will prevent us from experiencing the joy that Jesus promises his disciples if they live by his Word. We will find ourselves scattered and disjointed. It may very well be failure in this area above all else that robs postcollege Christians of joy and satisfaction with their lives.

Foster distinguishes between inner simplicity and outer simplicity. It does no good to pursue outer simplicity (living and eating without spending much money, avoiding extravagances and comfort-oriented gadgets, enjoying and preserving nature, and so on) without an inner focus. All our efforts are asceticism without purpose. But if we are pursuing God's kingdom and his righteousness first, we may buy things or not buy them, based not on legalistic criteria of simplicity-holiness but on our goals and the proper means to achieve them. We will reject many purchases as unnecessary extravagances. We will purchase some things for their usefulness to the kingdom. Decisions regarding these things will not be fraught with guilt or lust or regret but with joy in the chance to love God and serve others better.

One year nine of us moved into a house with five bedrooms. We were all involved in ministry together, and we were working at developing community in our relationships with one another. Because of age and experience, I was the leader of this household (and the new owner of the house). Given the mathematics of the situation, I could have asked to have the single room as my own. Instead, as a household we decided to set aside one bedroom as a guest room. That meant one of the four remaining rooms had to hold three people. As it turned out, relationally it made sense for me to share the triple with two other guys. At age twenty-seven I was living in a room with two roommates, and I loved it! If this sounds odd, that's only because of our cultural assumptions regarding the need for privacy.

The choice of hospitality over privacy is an example of simplicity. Simplicity means preferring the purposes of the kingdom of God to personal comfort. Simplicity yields resources mobilized for the kingdom of God, and it also yields the experience of joy contradicting any sense of sacrifice.

Referring again to the example at the beginning of the chapter, the choices Glenn and Matt have made have left them embracing simplicity very easily. Because of the size of their apartment, they simply cannot accumulate a lot of stuff. And because of the potential of theft, they are discouraged from buying expensive things. On the other hand, Matt recently purchased a second car, an old van, from a friend at church. While a second car in a city is something of an extravagance, the van fits into Matt's *simple* (that is, single-focused) lifestyle. Matt bought the clunky but working van in order to be able to transport kids. On Bible study nights and at other times throughout the week, the car is repeatedly filled with and emptied of kids as Matt or Glenn shuttles their young charges around the city. The single focus of these young men's lives guides their purchasing choices and their attitudes toward the things they do have.

Justice and Compassion

Examining Jesus' surprising story of using money to make friends for the kingdom in Luke 16, we discovered that disciples love people and use money. In fact, there is much danger in inverting this principle. A few verses after the parable of the shrewd steward, Jesus tells another story to warn against the love of money and the neglect of people:

There was a rich man who was dressed in purple and fine linen and who feasted sumptuously every day. And at his gate lay a poor man named Lazarus, covered with sores, who longed to satisfy his hunger with what fell from the rich man's table; even the dogs would come and lick his sores. The poor man died and was carried by the angels to be with Abraham. The rich man also died and was buried. In Hades, where he was being tormented, he looked up and saw Abraham far away and Lazarus by his side. He called out, "Father Abraham, have mercy on me, and send Lazarus to dip the tip of his finger in water and cool my tongue; for I am in agony in these flames." But Abraham said, "Child, remember that during your lifetime you received your good things, and Lazarus in like manner evil things; but now he is comforted here, and you are in agony. Besides all this, between you and us a great chasm has been fixed, so that those who might want to pass from here to you cannot do so, and no one can cross from there to us." He said, "Then, father, I beg you to send him to my father's house—for I have five brothers—that he may warn them, so that they will not also come into this place of torment." Abraham replied, "They have Moses and the prophets; they should listen to them." He said, "No, father Abraham; but if someone goes to them from the dead, they will repent." He said to him, "If they do not listen to Moses and the prophets, neither will they be convinced even if someone rises from the dead." (Luke 16:19-31)

It is as if Jesus told this parable to illustrate the principle of his previous parable. Here is an example of someone who loved money rather than people and therefore had no one to welcome him into the eternal dwellings. The rich man had resources that he could have used to care for people around him. Specifically, Lazarus would gladly have eaten the scraps from his table. The rich man's wealth eventually failed when he died—all of his worldly wealth suddenly counted for nothing. He had failed to love God and love his neighbor. Being a child of Abraham (v. 25) and therefore expecting to enter heaven, he was tragically surprised to find himself in perpetual torment.

In his death the rich man discovered an eternal and uncrossable gulf. Yet this gulf was formed during his life. The gate and fence around the rich man's property were a physical picture of the yawning chasm. The rich man probably saw Lazarus at his gate every day, yet never did anything to help him. His complete lack of concern for Lazarus widened the gulf further. Perhaps if the rich man had made efforts to break down this economic and social barrier in his lifetime, he wouldn't have ended up on the wrong side of it in death.

As college graduates (or soon-to-be), we all have wealth and educational capital that places us in a position to identify with the rich man of this story. Jesus calls us, his disciples, to break down the gulf between rich and poor. As we make choices to direct our resources (time, money, professional training, spiritual gifts) toward the poor, we begin to break down the barriers. This is a part of striving for the kingdom of God:

☐ The kingdom of God is advanced in our own lives as we declare allegiance to God alone.

☐ The kingdom of God is advanced in the lives of the poor as they receive their material needs as coming from God's provision, not simply from the benevolence of nice people like us. What we ultimately want for the poor is not wealth or even justice but inclusion in the body of Christ and participation in the economy of God through the community of God's people.

The story of the rich man and Lazarus is unsettling, because it suggests that the requirement for admittance into heaven is simply to have suffered poverty while on earth. But when we read the story in the context of the entire chapter, the requirement is simply faith in God rather than money. "You cannot serve God and wealth," Jesus said (v. 13). The rich man served money by allowing it to control him. He did not invest in eternal treasure. Though in this world he was wealthy, in heaven he was bankrupt.

We could imagine a different end for the rich man. Suppose he had invited Lazarus in for a meal. As they talked, he would have noticed Lazarus's sores. The rich man might have asked about medical care. Lazarus might have said, "The clinic won't treat me." The rich man at first might have offered to pay, but also might have asked *why* the clinic wouldn't help him. Out of his concern for Lazarus, the rich man might have begun to do what he could so that Lazarus could get the medical care he needed. As Lazarus began eating regularly and gained access to medical care, his health would have improved. The rich man would have begun to see his wealth in a different light—in the light of the purposes of God on earth. If he had begun to use his earthly wealth differently, he might not have died impoverished in the eyes of God.

We too cannot live a life of faith in God if we use wealth of any kind to shield ourselves from the poor. So how can we cross the barriers?

☐ If you pursue professional training (education, medicine, law), make choices to use that training for the kingdom of God. If God has given you a desire to pursue medicine, for example, consider taking your training and skill to the poor in an urban or rural underserved setting or even overseas. This will probably affect what medical school you attend, the specialty you choose and the residency program you seek. (If you are planning to work among the poor in the long term but that hasn't affected your choices in the short term, you are deceiving yourself.)

☐ If you don't *know* any poor people, begin to take steps to put yourself in a place where you can get to know them. Personal involvement in the lives of others often begins to break down walls of isolation.

☐ It is beyond the scope of this book to talk at length about the process of racial reconciliation, but any effort to break down barriers of class will address issues of race as well. Regardless of your race or class background, pursue relationships that will help you face these issues personally. Also take time to read books that will help you understand the depth of the challenge and to find hope for your own process.[2]

☐ Don't enter into this alone but with a community of people who are called to break down walls of alienation between rich and poor. Glenn, Matt, Paula, Sandy and several others from their church have become a prayer and ministry team supporting one another as they cross language, racial and social barriers to communicate the gospel. For all of them, this partnership has been crucial to perseverance and joy in ministry.

Mobilizing Your Lifestyle

Now let's return to the list of questions at the beginning of the chapter. It would be possible to answer those questions and feel pretty good about how we are doing if we were aiming for 10 percent better than the average. We might take pride in being able to say,

☐ I spend less money on nice clothes and fancy restaurants than my non-Christian friends.

☐ I am only half as stressed out as my peers at work.

☐ I don't live in the most expensive part of town.

☐ I don't spend as much money on expensive vacations as my non-Christian friends do.

☐ I try to watch only the best programs on TV.

Yet what would our lives be like, and what would our satisfaction with life be like, if we could say, with Paul, "One thing I do"? "Forgetting what is in the past, every day I strive forward for God's kingdom for that day. All of my energy, time, money and thoughts are spent seeking God's kingdom in my own life and in the lives of people around me." What would that involve? What would be the result?

☐ Where I live, how I receive my income and the focus of my ministry and relationships would overlap more. This probably would mean less time spent commuting and more time pursuing and enjoying relationships. I probably would live with other people and might not have as much privacy as I would prefer, but these choices would foster a deeper experience of community.

☐ I wouldn't have to ration TV watching, because I would be doing more purposeful things most of the time. Even rest and restoration might take a more meaningful form than couch potatodom. Glenn and Matt, Paula and Sandy don't even have TV sets, and they don't feel the lack. Their lives are full, loving and being loved by the people around them.

☐ I wouldn't take on stress at work, because I know that my work is to strive for the kingdom of God, letting God take care of the needs and worries of the day.

☐ The discipline of prayer would be focused and purposeful. For Glenn, Matt, Paula and Sandy, daily personal prayer and regular corporate prayer really matter—they are routinely aware of a depth of needs that most of us feel only rarely. So discipline in prayer comes out of their own need for God and not some tenuous sense of duty to God.

*   *   *

Our lifestyles reflect our values. If our lifestyles are going to reflect a wholehearted striving for God's kingdom, perhaps we need to reconsider the answers to these lifestyle questions in light of Jesus' values and God's call on our lives. As we do so, the circles of concern of our lives will come more into focus, our lives will be simplified, and our joy will be multiplied.

■ For Reflection
God, Work, Community, Church and Lifestyle

☐ Draw a diagram like the one on page 144 describing your life.

☐ How are the various circles related to one another? How would you like that to change?

The Centered Life

☐ Can you say, "This one thing I do . . ."? How could your life

(community, church, work and lifestyle) be more focused on God?
☐ What lifestyle decisions would you need to make?

God's Economy and Our Resources
☐ What would have to change for you to view yourself as a steward of God's resources?
☐ What steps could you take now to use worldly wealth to invest in eternal friendships?

Generosity
☐ Do you have a line in your budget for generosity? Are there ways that the resources God has entrusted to your stewardship could be more shrewdly mobilized for his kingdom?
☐ Think about your car—are you willing to loan it out, give rides to people and so on? Are you willing to be slightly inconvenienced in order to help someone who needs to borrow a car or who needs a ride?
☐ What about your books, records, tapes—are you willing to *give* them to people who borrow them, rather than expecting them back? What would this reflect about the relative value you place on things and on people?
☐ What about your computer, tools, stereo equipment—are you willing to let others use your stuff? Do you get anxious that someone might break it? How attached are you to your possessions?

Hospitality
Evaluate your current (or anticipated) living situation regarding its potential for hospitality.
☐ Are your living room, dining room and kitchen clean and usable for entertaining? Are there enough comfortable chairs and furniture? Are these areas typically free of miscellaneous piles, laundry and dirty dishes? Would people enjoy hanging out in these rooms?
☐ Does your meal policy include a provision for guests? Do you have regular meals together as a household? Could someone just drop in and be invited for dinner? Would someone feel free to do that?
☐ Is your place close to public transportation (if in an urban area)

or easily accessible by car (if not)? How available is parking? Will your friends or the people you reach out to be likely to want to come to your place?

☐ Do you have space for overnight guests? How prepared are you to receive people without warning?

☐ Do you often have food available for snacks, spontaneous parties or casual gatherings?

☐ Do you have group games that are easy to learn and fun for a variety of people? How do you do at inventing or initiating participative activities that don't cost a lot of money?

Simplicity

☐ How would your life be improved if you lived more simply?

☐ What steps could you take to bring your life more in line with a single-minded pursuit of the kingdom of God?

☐ What are some outward expressions of simplicity your life can take on now? If you haven't graduated, how will that be more difficult when you do?

Justice and Compassion

☐ Jesus mentions two specific manifestations of the rich man's lifestyle of luxury: his beautiful apparel and his daily feasts. How have your spending patterns on food and clothing made it easier or more difficult for you to be generous with the poor?

☐ What opportunities exist for you to bridge the chasm separating rich and poor?

For Further Reading

Foster, Richard J. *Freedom of Simplicity.* San Francisco: Harper & Row, 1981.

Peterson, Eugene H. *A Long Obedience in the Same Direction.* Downers Grove, Ill.: InterVarsity Press, 1980.

8
Embracing a Lifestyle of Ministry

Consider the stories of three recent college graduates who have embraced a lifestyle of ministry.

David. God originally had very little to do with David's lifelong dream to become a doctor. But while David was in college, his involvement in a Christian fellowship renewed his faith and gave him a love for ministry. So after being admitted to medical school, he deferred his program for one year in order to continue in ministry with his college group. Now he is in medical school, leading a Bible study for med students. David seeks out one-on-one time with the members of this growing study, and he is helping several of them to become more serious disciples of Jesus even while they pursue a rigorous academic program.

While in college, David committed himself to regular involvement with a homeless shelter. He continues to have regular contact with the poor through a soup kitchen near his medical school, which is situated in an inner-city neighborhood. He hopes one day to become a surgeon and to take his skills and training into an underserved area, in a city or perhaps overseas. But David has not postponed investing in other people until after he finishes medical school. He says, "Activities like these help me keep perspective on why God has called me to medical school."

Jennifer. Fulfilling a longtime desire to work with preadolescents, Jennifer became a sixth-grade earth science teacher. Her ministry to kids is reflected in comments their parents bring back to her. They are grateful for the personal attention and care she gives. She is open with kids and available to them; she has been a source of strength to several girls when they suspected they were pregnant. Jennifer herself is from a broken home; this has given her a special compassion for and interest in kids from a similar background. She is passionate about her subject and finds satisfaction in helping kids to discover science and to enjoy school.

Jennifer has also been a junior-high youth leader for several years at her church; a few of the kids she sees daily in class are also in the youth group. Watching kids make meaningful decisions to follow Jesus has been exciting for Jennifer, since she didn't grow up in a church. She is gaining a vision for how kids can become disciples in a church context. Besides leading the Sunday school, Jennifer and her husband, Randy, have begun a weekly discipleship group with six eighth-graders. They invest other time throughout the week with individual kids and attend many of their plays and performances. They have also come to know some of the kids' families, entering more fully into their lives.

Dan. Dan graduated from college in 1989 as a speech communications major, and then he moved to Oakland to volunteer with Harbor House, a ministry to recent immigrants and other poor people. Having put himself through college by running a housecleaning business, Dan took his skills, tools and contacts and expanded his business to employ other people. Over two years Dan hired several teams of workers, mostly Latinos, each team with its own manager and regular customers. His hopes were (1) to give people relatively new to the work force the skill and discipline to succeed and (2) to be an active gospel witness to those he hired. Later he sold parts of the business to the team managers as each gained the skills necessary to run the operation. Two of these businesses continue to thrive, and Dan still supports his ministry through his own business.

Dan and several other volunteers with Harbor House have moved into an ethnically mixed apartment complex. After spending time getting to know some recent immigrant families, they began a discipleship group for Cambodian boys ages ten and eleven, trying to reach them before they made a choice to join a gang. The group involves seven kids and three leaders. Dan sees the kids quite often. He and his partners offer tutoring a couple of nights a week and have a Bible study on Friday night. The group attends church together and spends the whole day together on Sundays, with outings and activities after the service. Dan has specific goals for the kids: that they become Christians (a few have) and that they become productive members of their community. The group encourages hard work in school, obedience to parents and school authorities, and leadership development. Already Dan has seen the group make a real difference in the lives of the boys.

Definition of Ministry

The word *ministry* could be defined in many ways for many purposes, but for our purposes this definition will be most helpful:

Ministry:
spending our lives on others to direct them toward God.

The three people whose stories are told above are spending their lives on others to direct them toward God. None of them is in "professional" Christian ministry. But they all see their lives as vehicles for the advance of the kingdom of God, in themselves and in others.

This definition of ministry has several implications.

Ministry is God-directed, not self-directed. Our goal is not that people respond to us in awe of our self-sacrifice but that they respond in awe of the great God who provides for us. Our goal is not that people like us because we are so kind and giving but that people love God and trust him because he is so praiseworthy and trustworthy.

Ministry is God-directed, not simply other-directed. Jesus says that to spend your life on any other cause than the advance of the gospel is a waste (Mark 8:34-35). Even spending your life in service of others with no thought for the kingdom is a waste according to Jesus. Many people do good deeds but ultimately lose their lives. Their good deeds testify to their own greatness, not God's. Only those who lose their lives for Christ's sake, relying on *his* strength and guidance, gain the promised eternal life.

Ministry can take a variety of forms. Evangelism, social justice, compassion, service, teaching and training, accountable relationships within Christian community—each has as a goal that the people we serve move closer to God, see Jesus more clearly, follow him more fully. Some ministry strategies may be more effective than others, measured on certain scales. But it is possible to spend your life helping others to grow toward God in a thousand different ways.

Specifically, ministry is not simply verbal communication. It certainly involves that, but getting people to "know" certain propositional statements is not our only goal. Simply speaking the truth apart from loving people enough to spend ourselves for them can be dangerous for us and for others. Unfortunately, much "ministry" is carried out without the love necessary to validate it, and the recipients of this "ministry" often feel angry and resentful.

Christian community is both a source and a destination of our ministry in the world. It is a *source* in that it fuels our ministry—gives us energy for it and gives it momentum and vitality. Community provides us with encouragement and partnership and clarity of vision. But this community is also a *destination* or goal of our ministry. Paul was told to convert Gentiles so they would receive forgiveness and a place among those sanctified by faith in Jesus (Acts 26:18). If people are properly directed toward God, they will be directed toward the body of Christ. No ministry is complete until people take their place in the body of Christ, which will help them continue to grow up into the full stature of a mature Christ-one.

Ministry is a total life involvement. We spend our *lives,* not simply a little bit of money, an hour or two of time, or one week per year. Ministry involves the full circle of our lives—our lifestyle choices, our work, our church and Christian community—all of our lives centered on God and the advance of his kingdom in us and in the lives of others around us.

The Blessings of Ministry

In the middle section of the Gospel of Mark Jesus teaches his disciples about the paradoxes of life in the kingdom of God. Jesus understands and sympathizes with his disciples' fundamental motives and drives. Peter at one point tells Jesus to save his life; Jesus responds with a paradox showing how life is really to be gained. Later Peter is feeling insecure because he has left everything to follow Jesus; Jesus responds with a paradox showing how we find true security. Later still the disciples are arguing about which of them is the greatest; Jesus responds with a paradox showing how true greatness is achieved.

He called the crowd with his disciples, and said to them, "If any want to become my followers, let them deny themselves and take up their cross and follow me. For those who want to save their life will lose it, and those who lose their life for my sake, and for the sake of the gospel, will save it. For what will it profit them to gain the whole world and forfeit their life? Indeed, what can they give in return for their life?" (Mark 8:34-37)

Jesus said, "Truly I tell you, there is no one who has left house or brothers or sisters or mother or father or children or fields, for my sake and for the sake of the good news, who will not receive a hundredfold now in this age—houses, brothers and sisters, mothers and children, and fields with persecutions—and in the age to come eternal life. But many who are first will be last, and the last will be first." (Mark 10:29-31)

So Jesus called them and said to them, "You know that among the Gentiles those whom they recognize as their rulers lord it over them, and their great ones are tyrants over them. But it is not so among you; but whoever wishes to become great among you must be your servant, and whoever wishes to be first among you must be slave of all. For the Son of Man came not to be served but to serve, and to give his life a ransom for many." (Mark 10:42-45)

Life. Security. Greatness. The astonishing thing in each case is that Jesus doesn't scold his disciples for wanting these things. He doesn't say, "You shouldn't care about saving your life!" "Christians don't need security!" "You shouldn't want to be great!" Rather, he actually appeals to their desire for these things but redirects their energies. "If you *really* want to save your life, lose it!" "If you want *true* security, leave everything that represents security[1] and follow me." "If you want *lasting* greatness, you must become a servant." These are fundamental motivations—we all desire these things. Jesus appeals to us, as he did to his disciples, to obey him and live the way he did in order to satisfy our deepest desires.

The path to life involves spending our lives on others for the sake of the gospel. The only lasting security is found as we throw our lot in with those who follow Jesus. We experience true greatness as we become servants of others in Jesus' name. Ministry is the paradoxical path to the satisfaction of our deepest longings. The apostle Paul understood this. He tells us why he lives the way he does, becoming a servant to any and all: "I do it all for the sake of the gospel, so that I may share in its blessings" (1 Corinthians 9:23).

Jesus' invitation to become a servant, a minister of the gospel, is conditional: only those who want to be great need bother to become a servant. We all want the things Jesus talks about. So why do we hesitate? What gets in our way? Let's consider some of the common obstacles to ministry and look at what Scripture has to say about them.

Obstacles to Ministry

Perhaps at one time or another you have heard, thought or even said one of the following statements:

☐ "I don't have energy for ministry."

☐ "I'm in transition and can't give myself to new relationships."

☐ "I have to work on my own problems before I am ready for ministry."

☐ "I am afraid of becoming burned out."

☐ "I don't have time—my schedule is too booked as it is."

☐ "I don't know what my gifts are."

How does Jesus respond to these statements? Somehow, if the paradox promises are true, then choices to give priority to ministry should yield a return. Life, security, greatness, joy: we know Jesus promises these things. So let's briefly examine these obstacles and hear the words of Jesus in response.

Ministry is sustenance. On a hot, dusty desert day at noontime Jesus' disciples are concerned for his health and urge him to eat. But he tells his disciples that ministry itself sustains him.

> Meanwhile the disciples were urging him, "Rabbi, eat something." But he said to them, "I have food to eat that you do not know about." So the disciples said to one another, "Surely no one has brought him something to eat?" Jesus said to them, "My food is to do the will of him who sent me and to complete his work. Do you not say, 'Four months more, then comes the harvest'? But I tell you, look around you, and see how the fields are ripe for harvesting." (John 4:31-35)

Jesus calls his disciples to see life the way he does. He says, "Look around you and see" all the people who are ready for the gospel. The disciples could literally turn and see; as Jesus spoke these words, a crowd from a nearby Samaritan town was being led to him by a woman with whom he had been speaking a few minutes before. Jesus himself is energized by the chance to see the dynamic spread of the kingdom of God. He gains energy as the gospel is proclaimed and people show interest. The disciples are concerned only about food for their journey; Jesus wants his disciples to be sustained the way he is, by doing God's will and completing his work. Jesus wants his disciples to live and thrive on striving for the kingdom of God.

It is indeed possible to live this way today. I expect that most reading this book have experienced the *food* of doing God's will. How many times have you heard someone report regarding a summer mission trip, "We went over there to serve in God's name, yet we received more from them than they did from us"? Repeatedly we are surprised that we are served by God even as we serve others in his name. As we give of ourselves to others, God supplies us with his strength, peace and joy.

This then is the economy of God: as we serve others in Jesus' name and with his resources, (1) God is glorified, (2) others' needs are met and they are directed toward God, and (3) we receive joy, peace, strength and more resources with which to continue to serve. If we are not experiencing this economy, we probably are not drawing on the resources of God. At such times ministry becomes draining and exhausting, and we may very well not have enough energy to do it.

We should *expect* to receive from God as we enter into ministry. God doesn't call us into ministry at the expense of our spiritual life. We shouldn't enter into ministry situations where the conditions are likely to be costly to us in the longest run. If this seems likely, probably something is wrong—either our attitude toward the situation or the situation itself. Often a lack of partnership and accountability is especially dangerous, making pride or abuse of authority more likely. Jesus always delegated ministry responsibilities, even simple tasks, to pairs of disciples. Amazingly, the only time the Gospels record any of Jesus' disciples doing anything alone was when Judas betrayed Jesus. Be wary of entering into solitary ministry situations!

Ministry is mobile. During the years right after graduation from college it can seem that your life is in such transition that you need to delay involvement in ministry. Yet if we have responded to Jesus' call to be his disciples, we are called to a life of ministry in the midst of our transition.

> He called the twelve and began to send them out two by two, and gave them authority over the unclean spirits. He ordered them to take nothing for their journey except a staff; no bread, no bag, no money in their belts; but to wear sandals and not to put on two tunics. He said to them, "Wherever you enter a house, stay there until you leave the place. If any place will not welcome you and they refuse to hear you, as you leave, shake off the dust that is on your feet as a testimony against them." (Mark 6:7-11)

Sending his disciples out to nearby villages, Jesus told them to travel light and be prepared to move around, but when they arrived in a town that welcomed them, they were to stay in one place and develop relationships there. If Jesus were speaking to us today, he might say, "I know you will feel unsettled the next few years and may live in four different apartments in as many years, but wherever you are, *invest in relationships there.* Get involved in ministry there until I call you to move on."

If we wait for the transition to be over, we may never get involved in ministry. By the time the transition is over (if it ever is), our lives may have become so comfortable and settled that we won't want to orient them toward ministry. Don't wait until you get into that graduate-school program, or until you finish! Don't wait until you pay off your school loans. Don't wait until you get married. Invest in ministry relationships where you are. God will lead you when it is time to move on.

Ministry puts problems in perspective. Some people are tempted to think that their problems are so consuming and confusing that they have no energy or ability to enter into ministry relationships. They assume that problems, weaknesses and sinful patterns all have to be eradicated before they take on ministry. Yet that is not how people grow up as disciples of Jesus. Paul gives a different model in Ephesians 4:

So then, putting away falsehood, let all of us speak the truth to our neighbors, for we are members of one another. Be angry but do not sin; do not let the sun go down on your anger, and do not make room for the devil. Thieves must give up stealing; rather let them labor and work honestly with their own hands, so as to have something to share with the needy. Let no evil talk come out of your mouths, but only what is useful for building up, as there is need, so that your words may give grace to those who hear. And do not grieve the Holy Spirit of God, with which you were marked with a seal for the day of redemption. Put away from you all bitterness and wrath and anger and wrangling and slander, together with all malice, and be kind to one another, tenderhearted, forgiving one another, as God in Christ has forgiven you. Therefore be imitators of God, as beloved children, and live in love, as Christ loved us and gave himself up for us, a fragrant offering and sacrifice to God. (Ephesians 4:25—5:2)

In the larger context of these verses Paul is challenging the Ephesians to get beyond their moral and spiritual problems. Paul says that they were taught "to put away your former way of life, your old self, corrupt and deluded by its lusts, and to be renewed in the spirit of your minds" (vv. 22-23). To show them how to do this, Paul gives these rules for a new life, mostly paired commands modeled after the "put off, put on" command. The negative command in each pair involves a character issue in the lives of the people, while each positive command involves a call to ministry:

☐ "let all of us speak the truth to our neighbors"

☐ "let [thieves] labor and work honestly with their own hands, so as to have something to share with the needy"

☐ "[only speak] what is useful for building up, as there is need, so that your words may give grace to those who hear"

☐ "be kind to one another, tenderhearted, forgiving one another"

☐ "live in love, as Christ loved us and gave himself up for us"

The fact is that a call into ministry is often exactly what we need to get beyond our problems, addictions, temptations and fears. In a sense Jesus' words to the man at the pool in John 5 are his words to us. He asks the man, "Do you want to be healed?" The man gives his excuses regarding why he hasn't been healed for so long. But Jesus simply says to him, "Get up!"

Sometimes a focus on our problems can actually paralyze us. Jesus wants us to get beyond them by taking our focus off ourselves and calling us to see the needs of others. Each of us can find people who are worse off than we are and offer them something in God's name. Our own healing will come as we begin in humility to look not to our own interests but to the interests of others.

In fact, entering into ministry often shakes up our schedule and priorities enough that some problems or temptations simply get squeezed out of our lives. This happens in romantic relationships or friendships marred by exclusivity and idolatry. As the two people enter into ministry, the best part of the relationship gets better, while the worst parts (exclusivity, sexual temptation and so on) they no longer have time for. While entering into ministry is not an easy solution to all problems, it is often a part of the process of moving toward a more spiritually healthy lifestyle.

Ministry with Jesus prevents burnout. We may be tempted to avoid ministry because we have had experiences of ministry that have led to burnout. Or we may have been in ministry and are "taking a break" in order to prevent burnout. But this attitude toward ministry is one of the surest ways to *produce* burnout.

The clearest example of burnout in the Gospels comes after the feeding of the five thousand, when the disciples row all night. When Jesus comes out to them walking on the water, their hearts are so hardened that they fail to recognize him: they think he is a ghost! The process leading to burnout began earlier that day, when Jesus promised his disciples rest after they had returned from their preaching tour of the cities of Galilee. Instead of finding a deserted retreat place, they found a crowd of people waiting for them. The disciples' hearts were hardened because of their sarcastic and resentful response to the ministry opportunity Jesus presented to them: "You give them something to eat." Jesus was trying to give the disciples the eyes of a shepherd, wanting them to see the crowds as he did: "They were like sheep without a shepherd" (Mark 6:34). But the disciples wanted Jesus to send them away; after all, they thought, he had promised them rest. Feeding five thousand people didn't sound like rest to them.

But I think that is exactly what Jesus had in mind. He wanted them to learn that rest and ministry aren't incompatible. If the disciples had had a different attitude, the whole experience could have been very exhilarating and rejuvenating. How exciting it could have been to listen to Jesus' teaching and then to see so many fed with so little and to participate gladly in the miracle. Instead their hearts were hardened. In their attempt to cling to Jesus' promise of rest, they failed to trust in Jesus. In their desire to be renewed after a time of intensive ministry, they missed the chance to be renewed through a rewarding experience of ministry.

Of course not all ministry opportunities are equally valid. Perceiving a need does not mean receiving a call. Some situations are more likely than others to result in burnout. But one certain way to burn out is to resist and resent Jesus' call into ministry out of fear of burnout.

Reexamining the stories that opened the chapter, we might worry that Jennifer could be prone to burnout: she has been in the same ministry (church youth leader) for five years, and she teaches the same age group in her work. Wouldn't she get tired of junior-highers? One day she may, but now she is experiencing partnership and satisfying ministry and is being renewed by God through the process. She hasn't decided to "take a break" out of fear of burnout; she presses ahead because she doesn't want to miss out on what God has for her.

A pruned life is a fruitful life. Jesus does not want us to be burned out in ministry. In fact, he calls us to live in a way that is deeply satisfying. He wants us to experience a meaningful and purposeful life.

I am the true vine, and my Father is the vinegrower. He removes every branch in me that bears no fruit. Every branch that bears fruit he prunes to make it bear more fruit. You have already been cleansed by the word that I have spoken to you. Abide in me as I abide in you. Just as the branch cannot bear fruit by itself unless it abides in the vine, neither can you unless you abide in me. I am the vine, you are the branches. Those who abide in me and I in them bear much fruit, because apart from me you can do nothing. . . .

You did not choose me but I chose you. And I appointed you to go and bear fruit, fruit that will last, so that the Father will give you whatever you ask him in my name. (John 15:1-5, 16)

A grapevine needs to be pruned so that the energy of the plant does not get consumed in producing a lot of branches and leaves. A plant can appear vigorous and vital because of its many leaves but be so dedicated to leaf growth that it produces a pitiful quantity of small, sour fruit. So the wise vinegrower will prune back the vine, allowing the plant to focus its sap on the remaining branches and the developing fruit.

Surprisingly, the pruning process is somewhat arbitrary. Sometimes it is sick branches that are pruned away, but often the cutting back is simply random. The trimmed branches weren't harmful in themselves—they simply took away energy from the fruit-bearing activity of the plant.

Jesus says we are like branches of the vine. Our lives are meant to be fruitful, but that involves pruning—allowing God to channel our time and energy toward the commitments and activities that will be most fruitful. The logic of our culture is to fill the emptiness of fundamental purposelessness with an abundance of activity. Our days are filled with busyness that seems critical at the time but on an eternal scale withers away to insignificance. Our nights are filled with club meetings, hobbies, church events and TV shows. Our weekends are filled with a relentless pursuit of recreation and a drivenness to enjoy our leisure time. All of these things are like leaves on the vine. They fill our time with activity, and from a distance our lives look healthy and vital. Yet with all the energy going into sheer activity very little is directed toward developing fruit.

David, the medical student who is pursuing ministry (see the beginning of this chapter), is probably as busy as anyone. But he makes time in his schedule for the ministry involvements he has chosen, and he is not the loser for it. He has less time to study, but his ministry involvements put all of his time into perspective.

Jesus says he wants our lives to bear lasting fruit, eternal fruit. "Heaven and earth will pass away," he says, but human beings are eternal. The only activity with potential for eternal fruit is investment in the lives of people. Ministry—spending our lives on others to direct them toward God—is the fruitful activity that should fill our lives.

If you don't have time for ministry, your life is too full. Don't allow even good things to get in the way of spending your life to have eternal impact on other people.

Discovering gifts through ministry. Perhaps you feel ready to get involved in ministry but haven't really identified what your gifts are. It's easy to think this way after leaving the convenient structures of campus ministry involvement while finding no obvious replacement.

Surprisingly, when Jesus called his band of disciples together, he seemed to disregard their specific gifts and personalities in favor of a one-experience-fits-all model. He told each of them, "Follow me and I will make you fish for people." He promised that they would become something they were not. When he sent them out two by two, he gave the Twelve only one set of instructions. Yet over time their personalities, gifts, sensitivities and talents emerged to give different shape to their ministries. Peter and John had almost the same amount of exposure to Jesus, but their different temperaments and gifts led them into ministry in different ways and to different groups of people.

Several years ago a half-dozen new college graduates moved into a house in an economically depressed and racially mixed neighborhood only a few miles from their college campus. They all found part-time work and spent the rest of their time building relationships with kids. They started three Bible clubs. Over time more graduates joined them. While the group began with a single leader, eventually other leadership roles were formed and a variety of ministries were begun, including after-school tutoring and a summer day camp. As the ministry grew and as those involved grew personally, their roles were further differentiated: some focused on older kids, others on children; some worked mostly in a predominantly Latino apartment building, others with African-American kids. Some worked part-time jobs, some worked full-time jobs. Some focused on group interaction, others gave priority to one-to-one friendships with children. Some were better teachers, others were better administrators. Some were motivated by the big vision, others were meticulous and faithful in the details. Several became full-time staff of this newly incorporated nonprofit, and fundraising became an added responsibility for them.

The reality is that if each of these people had waited for the perfect ministry role to come along before jumping into ministry, they might still be waiting today. Instead they all joined a ministry that they knew was something of a risk, and over time it paid off. They all had a desire to work with kids, but certainly not all of them were naturally gifted as youth workers. As time went on, each of them gained a greater confidence in their gifts and contribution to the team.

Jesus calls each of us to follow him and to fish for people. As we join him and enter into the work he is doing, we will grow in an understanding of our specific ministry gifts and interests. Then, as opportunities develop, our greater self-understanding will help us to discern God's leading.

Ministry, Evangelism and Community

In the first section of this chapter I said that small group Christian community is both a source and a destination of ministry. The challenge of ministry is to put our resources to work to give others greater confidence in God so that they draw near to him. An experience of satisfying Christian community gives us resources upon which to draw and gives us a tangible direction toward which to encourage those we minister to.

When this kind of ministry happens with people who are not yet Christians, we call it evangelism. When the process happens with Christians, we call it discipleship. Yet it is the same process. Our goal is the same: that people will draw near to God and find their greatest desires met in him, in part through the tangible expression of the body of Christ.

But I want to extend the relationship between community and ministry a little further. Community is not only the source and the destination of ministry but also the most effective ministry tool. The chapter opened with three personal stories. Not surprisingly, David, Jennifer and Dan (along with millions of other people involved in ministry) have focused their efforts on small groups of people, whether kids or medical students. A community of people gathered in Jesus' name is the most effective tool for shaping, developing, training and encouraging the spiritual growth of mature disciples, new believers or people who aren't yet Christians. It is the tool both Jesus and Paul used, to great effect. It is a tool we have available to us as well.

Imagine a small group of disciples who are trying to reach out to their non-Christian friends. Suppose each of them reaches out to two friends in a one-to-one strategy. Each group member tries to invite these friends to the small group of Christians. When the non-Christian friends arrive, they look around the room and each knows only one person, the friend who invited him or her. This makes the group dynamic difficult, and unless relationships form quickly, the non-Christian may be too uncomfortable to come back.

Now imagine a different strategy in which the community is seen as a tool for evangelism, not simply the final destination after success has been achieved. The small group discusses and prays for a list of people who are all known by more than one group member. In subgroups of two or three, group members spend time with these friends, demonstrating the love of Jesus. When responsive people are invited to the small group, they show up and find that they already know several members. In a sense they have been invited into the community, and that itself is an attractive part of the evangelism process. As one former atheist said to a group doing this kind of evangelism, "Your love for one another is the strongest proof I've seen for the existence of God." Shortly thereafter he became a Christian.

A ministry that is only feeding people with no concern to give them the gospel is incomplete (and vice versa). Likewise, if a ministry is focusing on evangelism but not on bringing people into a community of believers, it is incomplete. Evangelism and discipleship have as their goal that people be brought into deeper relationship with God. And that happens, as we see repeatedly in Scripture, only as people are brought into meaningful relationship with the body of Christ, the community of faith that together is striving for the kingdom of God.

■ *For Reflection*
Definition of Ministry
☐ How does your life reflect the priority of ministry?
☐ Who are the people you are spending your life for in order to direct them toward God?

The Blessings of Ministry
☐ Have you seen the paradox promises hold true in your own life?

How have you found life, security and greatness by choosing to give them up?

☐ How do you struggle with that now?

Obstacles to Ministry

☐ Which of these obstacles to ministry are relevant to you?

lack of energy for ministry

transition and unavailability for new relationships

personal problems preventing ministry

fear of burnout

lack of time—an overbooked schedule

uncertainty regarding ministry gifts

☐ What changes in your life would be necessary to break through these obstacles?

☐ Where can you get the resources you will need?

Ministry, Evangelism and Community

☐ How have you seen community serve

as a *source* of evangelism? (as the encouragement and impetus for outreach)

as a *destination* of evangelism? (as the place to which you drew people)

as a *tool* for evangelism? (as the means by which people were attracted to the gospel)

For Further Reading

Stevens, R. Paul. *The Equipper's Guide to Every-Member Ministry.* Downers Grove, Ill.: InterVarsity Press, 1992.

9
Finding God's Will for Your Life

The movie *The Blues Brothers* offers a tongue-in-cheek portrayal of divine guidance. Jake and Elwood Blues, played by John Belushi and Dan Aykroyd, are two grown men who deeply disappointed the nun ("the Penguin") who raised them in a Chicago orphanage. These men turned out bad. After Jake is released from prison, he returns with Elwood to hear from "the Penguin" that the orphanage will be closed unless five thousand dollars is raised to pay the tax assessment on the building. Jake offers to steal the money, but "the Penguin" will not receive stolen funds, and she chases them out of her office, telling them not to return until they have "redeemed themselves."

Jake and Elwood feel a certain affection for "the Penguin" and the orphanage janitor, the only family they have. They want to help but don't know what to do. Then they receive their "call from God" while attending an African-American church service. During the particularly rousing preaching/singing/dancing, a directed beam shines in through a high window onto Jake, and he "sees the light": he and

Elwood are to revive their old blues band and put on a concert in order to raise honest money for the orphanage. This revelation is the unlikely but entertaining premise for the rest of the movie, which ends with the entire band in jail but with the tax assessment being paid minutes before it was due. Throughout the movie, as Jake and Elwood pursue their quest in the face of many obstacles, they confidently reiterate, "We're on a mission from God."

We all want to feel we are "on a mission from God." Who wouldn't want to have a sense that God had appeared to them and appointed them to do something purposeful and specific, something with his stamp of approval and his promise of success? Yet most of us must consider and make all of our decisions, from the trivial to the weighty, without receiving God's specific, personal, voice-in-the-clouds type of guidance. Nevertheless, given all that we have seen in Scripture regarding the big decisions of life, we can expect God's hand to be at work.

Just Do It!

One day a graduating senior, full of hope and possibilities, came to Jesus and asked him, "Jesus, what is God's will for my life? I just want to do whatever God wants me to do."

Jesus, characteristically responding to a question with a question, replied, "You've done Bible study; how do you read it?"

The woman, taken aback only momentarily, recovered and said, "You mean, 'love God' and 'love your neighbor'?"

Jesus replied, "Yeah, that's how I read it too. Just do it."

The woman saw through this simple, naive, almost trite response. She wasn't about to let Jesus off that easily. She didn't want to look like an imbecile in front of the other graduating seniors waiting in line to ask Jesus for advice. "Just do it? It's much more complicated than that! Jesus, you fail to grasp the intricacy of the question." Having regained her composure, she paused, then added slowly, emphasizing each word, *Exactly who is my neighbor?*"

At this point, Jesus told the young woman a story of a man who was beaten, robbed and left for dead in a back alley, and of an illegal alien who stopped to help him and nurse him back to health. It was a shocking story, a very modern story, complete with random violence, subtle racism, an unlikely hero, religious villains and extravagant love. Though the woman had heard this story in Sunday school a thousand times, somehow she heard it as she never had before. She was caught up in the powerful images that Jesus' stark words portrayed.

She stared at Jesus, taking nothing in for a moment, until she realized that he had asked her a question. She snapped out of it. "Uh, what was that? Could you repeat the question?"

Jesus restated his question: "Which of the characters in the story acted as a neighbor to the man who was beaten and robbed?"

The woman, beginning to feel ashamed, replied, "The one, I guess, who showed mercy."

Jesus' patient, loving, simple reply came to her: "Do this and you will live."

Of course this story, taken from Luke 10:25-37, originally involved a lawyer, not a graduating senior. But other than that the details are pretty much the same. Both the lawyer in Luke and the woman above were interested in knowing God's will for their lives. And both were somewhat insulted by Jesus' implication that the answer is rather straightforward.

We want to think that we would gladly do God's will, if we only knew what it was. Since we don't know, we stand still, paralyzed that we might do something that's not part of God's game plan. Or we proceed as if God's will and the prudent choice were one and the same, unless we hear something contradictory directly from God. One way or the other, we think, "The hard part is knowing God's will; if I only knew God's will, doing it would be easy."

We are just like the lawyer. The lawyer didn't want to waste his precious time and resources loving people who didn't count in the "neighbor" category. So he wanted Jesus to get more specific. "Love your neighbor" is too vague. "I want categories! I want limits! I want rules! Who's the neighbor? Is it all educated people? Is it all needy people in my city? Is it all the homeless? All the 'deserving poor'?"

We pray to God, "Let me know your will and I will follow you." Yet we don't learn God's will and then examine it, weigh it, considering whether to follow it.

Suppose God appeared one morning at the foot of your bed as your alarm was about to go off and said, "I want you to prepare to become a missionary to Japan. I have great things planned for you there." This kind of experience would impress upon you the need to prepare to go as a missionary to Japan. Perhaps this is what we hope for when we pray these words: "Let me know your will, God." God doesn't work that way in our lives very often. But he *has* revealed much about his will.

Think about the difference between the lawyer's question and Jesus' question. The lawyer asked, "Who is my neighbor?" Jesus asked, "Who was a neighbor to the man?" The lawyer's question focused on obligation, seeking a limitation to the onerous command to love one's neighbor. Jesus' question focused on opportunity: "There was an opportunity to love this man as a neighbor; who seized the opportunity?" The lawyer's focus was right knowledge; Jesus' focus was right action: "Do this, and you will live."

None of us need to ask God, "God, is it your will for me to love people today?" He has made his will plain. It is neither complex nor confusing. He has only two main priorities for us: to love him and to love other people. The only question is the details, how it will be lived out. Actually we have it backwards. The hard part is not *knowing* God's will. It is *doing* what we already know *is* God's will.

Jesus affirms here, as we have seen before, that his two priorities in life were simple ones: to love his Father God and to love his neighbor. He calls us to live by these as well. What does he mean? These commands can be restated simply:

Love God = Trust God

Love others = Serve others

We love God by placing the whole of our lives in his hands, by trusting him entirely for all that we need, have and hope for. We love others by serving them in God's name, by spending our lives on others to direct them toward God. This is the summary of God's will for our lives.

What should the lawyer or the graduating senior learn from the story Jesus told? In the original story, the Samaritan knew whom to love because of two things: (1) he perceived a need—a person in real need crossed his path, and (2) he recognized that he had resources to care for this person in need. So he responded in love for his neighbor in need. The kind of love he offered was costly. It cost his resources: money and oil for the wounds, and he even picked up the man's hotel bill. It cost his comfort: the wounded man rode on his donkey while he had to walk down the hot, dusty road to the inn. It cost him time: all of the care the Samaritan gave the man took time from his busy schedule. Caring for this man didn't help the Samaritan get where he wanted to go. It cost him his racial prejudice—he chose to help a man from a race that considered him a dirty half-breed, truly less than human.

When we face choices with no clear "God's-voice" guidance, we can begin to eliminate some options and focus on others based on the opportunities to live by the priorities Jesus has for his disciples.

But this does not mean that God's will for all of us is exactly the same. We also need to take into account the unique way God has created us.

When I Run I Feel His Pleasure

The movie *Chariots of Fire* won the Academy Award for Best Picture in 1981. It is the story of the British running team in the 1924 Olympics, and particularly the story of two men, Eric Liddell and Harold Abrahams, both world-class runners but with very different motivations. Eric Liddell and his sister Jennie were Christian missionary kids who themselves were preparing for the mission field. At one point Jennie is worried because it seems that Eric has neglected his ministry and is spending all of his time preparing for the Olympics. One scene shows Jennie and Eric on a beautiful Scotland hill. Eric says, "Don't fret for me, Jennie."

She says, "I do fret for you, Eric."

Then Eric gives his memorable line: "Jennie, I know God has made me for a purpose, but he has also made me fast. And when I run, I feel his pleasure."

"I know he has made me for a purpose"—and it is not to win the Olympic gold medal. That is the implication. Eric is saying to his beloved sister, "Jennie, I am with you. I know God has made me for a purpose, and my whole life is given to it. I want to love God and love people as well as I know how." Eric Liddell went on to become a missionary in China, spending his life and dying there for the advancement of the gospel.

"But he has also made me fast, and when I run I feel his pleasure." What a great sentiment! Liddell takes enormous delight in running very fast. What a contrast to the drivenness of his rival Abrahams, who knows no peace as he runs, and who competes in a never-ending quest to prove himself.

When I taught computer science at Stanford University, I felt God's pleasure. I loved to get up in front of students, most of whom were somewhat afraid of computers, and begin to light a fire of interest in the subject. This was in the early 1980s, before personal computers were commonplace. Most of my students had their first real experience of computers in my class. I loved to spend late nights in the computer center with students as they worked on programming assignments due the next day. Whether from the front of the lecture hall before a hundred or looking over the shoulder of an individual—when I saw the spark of understanding in the eyes of students, I felt the pleasure of God.

I taught computer programming for three years as a part-time "tent-making" job to support my full-time but volunteer ministry to college students. I knew God made me for a purpose, to strive to advance the gospel in the lives of students. But he also made me a teacher and gave me skills to enable me to do it well, and he allowed me to thrill in teaching as I was exercising my God-given gifts. I was good at it, I enjoyed it, and ministry happened through it.

Eventually I decided that, as much as I enjoyed teaching computer programming, I enjoyed student ministry more, and I moved into a full-time position with InterVarsity Christian Fellowship. As I look back, it's clear that God used my experience of teaching programming and all that came out of it to prepare me for my current life and ministry, in which teaching still plays a central role. I didn't leave behind teaching as I left Stanford's computer science department. When I teach, I still feel God's pleasure.

God wants us to be free to enjoy the work we do, when work is understood in the sense of striving for God's kingdom. When we remove "making a living" from our notion of work (see chapter four), we begin to experience freedom to pursue what we enjoy. We don't want to be satisfied just making a living when we can be using our gifts and talents to strive toward the kingdom. Once that is our focus and desire, we can discover the kinds of things in which we feel God's pleasure and can pursue those things and trust God to guide us the rest of the way.

Let me get specific for a moment. You may be pursuing, as I once was, a high-status, high-income (and high-stress) job because of the material compensations and rewards. You are unlikely ever to experience "God's pleasure" if this is your purpose and desire. You may as well be honest with yourself. For example, if you enter law school simply because after three years you can expect to command a high salary and a respectable status, you will be the biggest loser. Is it God or your own pride and idolatry that has called you to law school?

On the other hand, God may have given you a desire to seek justice and an ability to think clearly and logically. God may have fashioned you in such a way that you could really enjoy law school and the profession of law. But don't forget that God made you for a purpose: to love him and to love other people. Use your skills to love others. An attorney can serve people in many ways and love them through skills made available in servanthood. Honor God by being generous with your earnings as you trust him alone for your provision and sustenance.

If we let go of cultural assumptions about what is supposed to make us happy (such as a status career or a high-income job), we can make choices that will bring us happiness as we do what God created us to do. And we can fulfill God's purpose in creating us and calling us to himself as we love him by trusting him and love others by serving them.

Most likely you will not go into "professional Christian ministry." Perhaps some people who are planning on it really should decide not to. Full-time, paid Christian ministry is the exception, not the rule. Choosing that path is not more noble or honored than making any other faithful choice. Some people may be unfaithful by not choosing to direct their lives toward full-time ministry, but others may be unfaithful by not channeling their love for God and others through doing carpentry, teaching in elementary school, piloting planes or being an accountant. For many people, parenting is the most satisfying ministry, job or work situation they experience, even though the culture doesn't place as much value on parenthood as on a paying career.

I hope all of us will be able to enjoy what we do with our lives. Yet some of us may do tentmaking work that does not allow us to taste "the pleasure of God" while on the job; our deepest satisfaction will come, as it did for Paul, in being able to minister the gospel freely. Many of us will have full-time jobs, at least for part of our lives. But may we not be satisfied until we "feel God's pleasure."

Lives That Don't Make Sense

A couple of chapters back I invited you into a "thought experiment" regarding money. Now I would like you to try another experiment. Imagine that a video camera is fixed on your life, recording for posterity all the major choices and decisions, all the turning points, the forks in the road. For the sake of peace of mind, let's assume that your nastier private sins are omitted from this videotape. This is a tape of your *public* history. The videotape includes sound but not thoughts, so everything an eyewitness would experience is recorded.

Now assume that we turn this (very, very long) tape over to an expert video editor. Her job is to remove any audio and video references to God, Jesus, your spiritual life and the Bible. The editor then returns the tape and we replay it, watching with eager anticipation as the events of your life unfold before our eyes.

What kind of a story would we see? Would the story line make sense? Would the choices you made and the path you took make sense? Would the viewer understand your choice of which college to attend? your choice of which job to take after college? your choice of where and with whom to live? the direction of your life? Consider your choices: are they completely predictable? You may think that they were motivated by God, but could someone looking at your life and choices on tape understand everything you've done on the world's terms alone?

This thought experiment reveals something of what a life of faith means. We should regularly be making choices that would be completely inscrutable apart from God. Like Abraham's choice to leave his homeland and go, not knowing where. Like Noah's choice to build a huge boat in the desert. Like Moses' choice to reject his adopted royal Egyptian heritage to identify with God's enslaved people. Like Peter's choice to leave behind the biggest catch of his life to follow Jesus. Like Eric Liddell's choice not to run in an Olympic heat on the sabbath, so that he was disqualified for the medal he prepared for two years to win.

We are meant to be confusing and confounding to those who don't acknowledge God's work in the world. If we can easily edit out fifteen minutes of prayer here and two hours of church or Bible study there and still make sense of our choices and motivations, then faith in God isn't much of a factor in our lives.

As followers of Jesus we are designed to live in such a way that if people filtered God out of our life's story, they would look at it and say, "This is crazy. This is senseless." Or to look at it in reverse, we are designed to live our lives so that people cannot reasonably filter God out of our story. We are meant to live in such a way that our lives provide undeniable testimony to the reality of a faithful God.

One way to make choices counting on God to work is to voluntarily limit your options. In the world this is always considered a foolish tactic. Russ, a Christian graduate, applied to several different programs at eight different graduate schools. On top of that he sent out résumés to twenty different firms in six cities across the United States. Russ was exploring future plans as if God were not in the picture at all. Sure, God could work by opening the right doors to get him into the right program or job. But how would Russ be sure that it was God, and not just the law of averages, that opened up a particular job or study program in a particular city? Some people have an idolatrous inclination to pursue a multiplicity of options as if God couldn't guide them through a limited set of options. Most people in the world would be happy with two options for the future.

Take risks and expect God to come through; don't plan your career with all sorts of contingency plans. Plan as if God must be present in your life, and you will not be disappointed.

This is not to be presumptuous or to test God. Don't assume he will get you into your preferred graduate school because you think he wants you in a certain program. While limiting your options, be ready for God to work through disappointment, not simply success. You may need to look for work, any work, if you do not get into the grad school of your choice. It may even be that God didn't want you in grad school. In that case rejection could be a form of God's mercy.

A Lamp to My Feet

Going to college often begins a process of making long-term plans and encourages having long-term aspirations. As you have probably found out, this process is only exaggerated as you prepare to graduate. Emphasis is placed on getting on the right *career track*. You are told to get on the *fast track*. Once you have a job, you are encouraged to get on the *management track*. With more education you could even get on the *executive track*. Lawyers get on the *partner track,* physicians the *specialist track,* academics the *tenure track*. Each of these tracks lays out your required choices and scheduled achievements, as well as specifying obstacles in your path. If you work hard, the promised rewards of these tracks will be yours in just a few years.

But as followers of Jesus, we need to be on the *discipleship track*. Following Jesus is what it implies, following someone who is moving. We need to have the same attitude toward Jesus' words that the psalmist did toward the Scripture available to him: "Your word is a lamp to my feet and a light to my path" (Psalm 119:105). God's Word is not a spotlight down the whole multidecade freeway of our lives; it's more

192

like a hand-held flashlight illuminating the next few steps on a narrow path. When we are on the discipleship track, we have received promises about our ultimate destination but no assurances about the path (other than that the way will be hard and few make it). So we have to stay close to the path as it is illuminated for us a step at a time by God's Word.

Some people are nearsighted and some are farsighted regarding their lives. Some people can only focus on the events of today. Next week is far off—forget about ten years from now! Others have vision for where they want to be in ten years but may be a little fuzzy on what God may want for them today. Whatever our vision problem may be, we need the helpful corrective lens of God's Word to give clarity as we look at the world and our choices. God's Word should shape the values by which we live daily as well as the long-term direction our lives will take.

One way to gain some clarity about God's design for your future is to reflect on past experiences that have prepared you for a particular work/ministry direction. If God used a youth ministry worker to touch your life while you were in high school, perhaps God is preparing you to work with high-school kids, either in a career as a teacher or as a volunteer through a church or parachurch ministry. Paula, one of the four whose story opened chapter seven, is an ethnic Chinese immigrant from Vietnam. This background gave her compassion for and a desire to work with people in need from a similar background. Her volunteer ministry to this group of people led her to find full-time work in a public agency addressing their needs. Another recent graduate, Karen, began to gain vision for ministry to prison inmates when her own brother was imprisoned.

We may be tempted to get off the discipleship track by trying to pay for present-day faithlessness with a promise of future faithfulness. We say, "God wants me to be a missionary, but first I must find a wife." Such a goal may be quite legitimate, but putting our faithfulness to God on hold creates a very real danger. We may easily be tempted to justify our present inconsistencies with the rationalization that in the future our lives will be more faithful. So we allow stinginess with our resources, an unavailability for ministry, sexual impurity or drivenness and anxiety at work to persist because we hope one day to make up for it with a heroic decision to yield our lives fully to God's will. Yet if we live this way today, we will be likely to end up nowhere near where he wants us later. Present faithlessness is no foundation for future faithfulness.

Paying off college loans. Alan graduated from college nearly twenty thousand dollars in debt. His loan payment was $232 per month for ten years. Alan thought of using his engineering training to secure a position in the Middle East as a tentmaking missionary, but he didn't feel ready to go until he had eliminated his debt. So he secured a good job, earning over thirty thousand dollars a year before taxes. He hoped to make payments of nearly one thousand dollars per month to pay off the loan in less than two years.

Alan found it hard to make payments as he'd hoped. His work schedule was grueling, so he ate out fairly often. His professional friends lived more extravagantly than he did, but he noticed that his tastes in food, entertainment and clothing were beginning to become more expensive. As his tastes changed, his spending on these things grew.

Eventually Alan forgot why he'd even wanted to go to the Middle East. He took a vacation trip to Asia, an area that was much more fascinating to him, but he never thought of becoming a missionary there. Alan did pay off his college loans early, after only four years. To celebrate, he purchased a new car (like those of his friends), with monthly loan payments slightly higher than his college loan payments had been.

Where did Alan's plans go wrong? Among other things, he lacked partners to hold him accountable to stay on track.

If you are graduating with several hundred dollars per month in loan payments, it may be a helpful goal to try to pay off your debts quickly so that you will be more available for ministry, especially overseas missions. But you will need to find partnership and support during this process. It's very easy to become trapped by upscale lifestyle choices when your income stream starts high and grows fast.

Finding Partnership

"It is not good that [anyone] should be alone" (Genesis 2:18). What was true for Adam in the Garden of Eden is as true for college graduates trying to discern God's will for their lives, or at least for the next step or two. It is not good to be alone. In each of the last five chapters we have seen how partnership is an essential foundation for faithfulness to the gospel. Partnership in the work setting will facilitate ministry there. Partnership is a necessary component of community and of a satisfying church experience. Partnership in faithful lifestyle choices makes those choices possible and more rewarding. Partnership in ministry fuels and renews those who are doing it. Partnership provides accountability in all these things. If you want to follow Jesus in these areas of your life, you will need to look for partners.

We tend to take partnership for granted and expect that finding a job is the real challenge of graduating from college. Rather the reverse is more likely: most jobs could lend themselves to striving for the kingdom, but finding satisfying partnership is surprisingly difficult. So we should make decisions that reflect the importance and the relative scarcity of partnership. If the limiting factor is partnership rather than jobs, that may have implications for the decision-making process.

Finding any kind of partner is a little scary. People are always less attractive in particular than in general. It is a lot like joining a church: we all want to find a church to which we can contribute and from which we can learn, but when we are confronted with real churches (and not simply the ideals we uphold), commitment becomes scary. Likewise with marriage: probably most of us want to be married (in general), but as we get to know someone specific, commitment can become a scary thing.

Partnership is confining. It requires us to say, "I'm willing to decide that my life and future will be affected by your choices." Whether in ministry, housing, job or marriage, commitment to real, flawed, sinful humans is scary because as we get to know people we will not like everything we see.

Of course the reverse is also true. We make ourselves vulnerable when we invite someone into our life enough to let them matter to us and to make plans around their choices. "Will you live with me?" is almost as vulnerable a question as "Will you marry me?" The fear of rejection can erode faith in God. We think, *What if mathematically it all works out for everyone else, but I am left out? What if God doesn't plan to give me the kind of partnership and experience of community that he generously gives to others?*

Above I suggested that to live as if God makes a difference might involve limiting our options rather than pursuing many different possibilities for life after college. One practical way to limit options is to decide to stay in or move to a certain location based on the church and meaningful partnership you would enjoy in that city. Consider deciding your location first, then look for a job (or apply to graduate school). It limits the options, but God's call on your life may be more to a group of partners than to a particular job or program in a far-off city.

I know two guys who decided to apply to the same graduate schools and made choices to attend the one that accepted them both. The world would understand this kind of self-imposed constraint in the case of a married or sexually involved couple. But for Christian friends who want to help each other be faithful after college, this kind of choice is a powerful testimony to the priority of God in their lives.

Probably the most difficult thing about finding partnership is making the transition from the possible to the definite. We look around at church or in a Christian group and think about people as potential partners. Having lots of possibilities is exciting. But our tendency is to postpone the point of commitment until all the pieces fall into place. It is as if everyone is waiting until everyone else is committed before they are willing to commit themselves. And no one is ready to be committed until all the pieces of his or her own life (job, housing, church, ministry) fall into place. So we all dance around each other, wanting to keep the others interested but preserving our own freedom from entanglement as long as possible.

This dance of ambivalence can derail God-inspired vision for partnership and community. I have seen this with groups interested in moving forward in ministry together, groups considering overseas missions together and groups looking for housing together. The way out of the commitment dilemma is also the way of faith. The challenge is to make a faithful decision without all the pieces in place.

Tim, a graduate student living in a household of people in ministry to undergraduates, had the vision to begin a similar household of graduate students. It was difficult to imagine leaving his very satisfying experience of household community unless he knew that he would be able to experience it again. Yet it would never happen unless he took the risk and committed himself to try. So Tim found another graduate student, Ken, and the two of them said, "We're in." Tim now had a partner, and the two of them began to talk with others about the kind of household community they were looking for. Tim's willingness to leave behind what was comfortable made all the difference: the graduate-student household formed around Tim and Ken's commitment and vision.

What would be the effect on your friends and partners if you were to say, "I'm in; how about you?" As you make that statement you testify to God's power to make the possible real. Faith is exactly that, "the conviction of things not seen" (Hebrews 11:1). This kind of faith calls out of others a response of hope, and before long what was unseen becomes tangible reality through the grace of God.

Discernment and Community

Is discernment essentially an individual's task? Is it true that even deciding that God is calling you into community with other people is an individual process? In fact, in a sense this is true. All of us need to decide for ourselves that we intend to follow Jesus, and each of us needs to personally own the decisions involved in living that out.

But very often in Scripture we see people making decisions *as* a group *for* the group, without a specific sense that the individuals came to the decisions independently. Paul and Barnabas were sent out as missionaries by the Antioch church as a result of a prayer time among the leaders. No time was wasted helping Paul and Barnabas come to agreement with the decision God's Spirit had revealed to the leaders in prayer (Acts 13:1-4). When Lydia was converted by Paul's persuasion, her whole household was baptized (Acts 16:15). Later the Philippian jailer was converted and his entire household was converted, all at once in the middle of the night (Acts 16:33). It is certainly not necessary to think that the other members of these households did not believe; rather, the decision was not at its core each individual's decision.

This kind of radical individual participation in the corporate means that the community will impinge on the plans and decisions of individual members. Certainly the community will make decisions regarding its corporate life, and these will impinge on individuals. But the community may also offer wisdom and counsel on upcoming decisions in the individual's life. It may even challenge and call into question decisions the individual has already made or is about to carry out. This is meaningful accountability and partnership in action.

A few years ago my wife and I were considering a cross-country move in response to a call to minister with InterVarsity at Harvard University. We were excited about the potential but aware of the cost of the move: the loss of community, the potential danger to our faith. We were a part of a team of IVCF staff who took their relationships with one another very seriously. As a team we spent two days praying about and talking through the option, one day in May and another in September.

In May our partners brought up a number of issues that we decided we needed to talk through with our prospective supervisor before we made the decision to move. In September, having heard the responses to these and other questions, the team became convinced that God was indeed calling us to go to Boston. This certainly confirmed our own sense of call to Boston and gave us the reassurance we needed, especially later, during a difficult first year of transition to the East Coast. Without the confirmation from our partners it would have been easy to doubt God's call when things became difficult.

My hope is that each graduating senior or recent graduate seeking God's will for his or her life will have and submit to the kind of community that can ask tough questions about plans, hopes, goals and the motives behind them. This community serves not simply to police insincere motives but also as a confirmation, to affirm our own sense of calling and to identify spiritual gifts and encourage their use.

■ *For Reflection*
Just Do It!

☐ What would it look like to think through decisions about your future in the light of Jesus' story about the good neighbor?

☐ Take an inventory of your gifts, abilities, interests and resources. How can they be used to love people?

☐ These same gifts and abilities, given by God, can become a snare and inhibit trust in God. How are you tempted to rely on yourself and your abilities for the things God has promised to provide as you strive for his kingdom?

☐ What would it look like to take a bold risk, a step of faith?

Don't wait until you know God's will perfectly, but simply do what you know. As you begin to move, God will guide you further. Make an effort to leave God freedom to bless your gifts for his service or to remove them as stumbling blocks in your life.

When I Run I Feel His Pleasure

☐ How would you express what you know about yourself in Eric Liddell's words: "God has made me _____ , and when I _____ I feel his pleasure"?

☐ How could this understanding of yourself guide you as you think about choices you have before you?

Lives That Don't Make Sense

☐ When was the last time you made a choice that, apart from God, made no sense at all? When was the last time you made a plan that, unless God were real and active, would surely fail?

☐ Have you ever experienced a closed option as mercy from God? How were you given perspective to see it in those terms? (Have you prayed in thanksgiving to God for his wisdom in closing a door you might otherwise have walked through?)

A Lamp to My Feet

☐ Is your own life vision nearsighted or farsighted?

☐ How could your vision be corrected?

☐ Do you have college loans to pay off? How quickly do you plan to pay them off? What help will you need to maintain your goals?

Finding Partnership

☐ Reflect on the nature of your current partnerships and your prospects for the future. Think about people who are currently meaningful partners to you:

in your job or academic setting

in your community or church

in your living situation

in ministry

☐ How could your effectiveness and satisfaction in these areas increase as your experience of meaningful partnership increases?

☐ If you lack partnership in one or more areas, whom could you approach to see if God could build partnership with them? What risks would it involve for you?

☐ What would it mean for you to say, "I'm in. How about you?"

Discernment and Community

☐ Identify decisions currently facing you in the following areas:

job, grad school, career

church and community

living situation and geographic location

lifestyle and the use of money

ministry

romance and friendship

☐ Which of these areas would be more or less difficult for you to allow your partners or community to be involved in?

☐ How have you submitted your decision-making process regarding any of these issues to the wisdom and accountability of your community?

☐ If you haven't already done so, what active steps could you take to seek out guidance and accountability?

For Further Reading

Smith, M. Blaine. *Knowing God's Will.* Downers Grove, Ill.: InterVarsity
    Press, 1991.

10
The Joy
of Obedience

Graduating from college is a little like competing in the Olympics. You train and prepare for years, with long days of practice and countless choices to postpone other gratifications in order to achieve your goal. You compete in and sometimes win smaller matches to qualify for ever more elite competition. Finally when your day arrives and you compete and win, you feel that release, that satisfaction, that . . .

Emptiness. The emptiness that comes when you realize that it was not the Olympics you were competing in but just the qualifying heats. The preliminaries. In fact, for you the Olympics aren't over, they have just begun and will take another forty or fifty years to complete. Sure, you've accomplished something, but the real test and validation of all your past effort is still in the future, the far-distant future.

It is almost impossible to sustain energy and movement toward lifelong goals. Only a few historical greats seem to have been able to do so. Certainly those of us who grew up on TV with its half-hour sitcoms have enough trouble mustering up an attention span for a six-hour miniseries, let alone working toward goals that are a lifetime in the making.

So we set intermediate goals: graduation from college, a trip to Europe, that first promotion, getting married, home ownership and so on. But unless we occasionally lift our sights and consider the trajectory of our lives, we may find in the end that we have accomplished little of eternal value over the course of our lives even though we succeeded in achieving all of our short-term goals in the process.

Let's listen to the apostle Paul one final time as he helps us set our sights on the things that matter most.

Press On Toward the Goal

The themes of Paul's letter to the Philippians make it a great choice for study for graduating seniors or recent graduates. Paul's main concerns about servanthood, partnership, perseverance and joy are critical for the transition time after graduation. Look now at some of his closing words to his beloved community:

Finally, my brothers and sisters, rejoice in the Lord.

To write the same things to you is not troublesome to me, and for you it is a safeguard.

Beware of the dogs, beware of the evil workers, beware of those who mutilate the flesh! For it is we who are the circumcision, who worship in the Spirit of God and boast in Christ Jesus and have no confidence in the flesh—even though I, too, have reason for confidence in the flesh.

If anyone else has reason to be confident in the flesh, I have more: circumcised on the eighth day, a member of the people of Israel, of the tribe of Benjamin, a Hebrew born of Hebrews; as to the law, a Pharisee; as to zeal, a persecutor of the church; as to righteousness under the law, blameless.

Yet whatever gains I had, these I have come to regard as loss because of Christ. (Philippians 3:1-7)

Paul calls the Philippians to "rejoice in the Lord," in contrast to those who rejoice in the flesh—those who take confidence in the outward marks of faithfulness to God, like circumcision. Paul is vehement here and elsewhere that there is nothing you can do that gives you favored standing with God. Those who took confidence in the works of the flesh thought that simple ritual observances earned points with God and obligated him to bless them. Paul gives the Philippians a stern warning against those who would foist this kind of legalistic religion on them.

Paul, a master debater, preempts one of his imagined opponents' responses. They might say, "Paul, you are just saying that you take no confidence in the flesh because you have no reason to take confidence in the flesh anyway." That would be like someone without a college degree saying college education is worthless. When an outsider to an elite system says the system is flawed, he or she cannot be taken seriously.

So Paul preempts their attack by claiming, "No, actually, if anyone is an insider to the 'confidence in the flesh' system, it is I." He goes on to list all his qualifications for critiquing the system. His ultimate qualification: "as to righteousness under the law, blameless." Rather than a critique of the system from one who couldn't make it, this critique comes from one who formerly excelled in the system. This stance gives Paul's warnings and evaluation added weight.

So Paul lists his credentials under the old system simply so he can junk the old system with authority. How does he feel now about his "flesh" résumé? He says he counts it all as loss. He speaks in accounting language. It as if he had been going over his books, feeling great about all of his accomplishments, summing their value: "$500,000! Wow, I'm rich!" And then, as God revealed to him the true value of his actions, he realized that the gain he thought he had was really loss. He discovered that the amounts weren't positive sums, but negative. A half-million surplus became a half-million deficit! He came to regard it as loss.

But Paul doesn't stop there.

More than that, I regard everything as loss because of the surpassing value of knowing Christ Jesus my Lord. For his sake I have suffered the loss of all things, and I regard them as rubbish, in order that I may gain Christ and be found in him, not having a righteousness of my own that comes from the law, but one that comes through faith in Christ, the righteousness from God based on faith. I want to know Christ and the power of his resurrection and the sharing of his sufferings by becoming like him in his death, if somehow I may attain the resurrection from the dead.

Not that I have already obtained this or have already reached the goal; but I press on to make it my own, because Christ Jesus has made me his own. Beloved, I do not consider that I have made it my own; but this one thing I do: forgetting what lies behind and straining forward to what lies ahead, I press on toward the goal for the prize of the heavenly call of God in Christ Jesus. Let those of us then who are mature be of the same mind; and if you think differently about anything, this too God will reveal to you. Only let us hold fast to what we have attained. (Philippians 3:8-16)

Here Paul continues to use the accounting metaphor to talk about how he views his past and his future. He regards everything as loss for the surpassing value of knowing Christ Jesus his Lord. In other words, he is not trading away something of surpassing value in order to get something of mediocre value. Rather, he trades away things he considers "rubbish" in order to receive something of surpassing worth. Hardly a difficult trade, from Paul's enlightened perspective.

His summary of this process is found in verses 13 and 14: "This one thing I do: forgetting what lies behind and straining forward to what lies ahead, I press on toward the goal for the prize of the heavenly call of God in Christ Jesus."

In an Olympic race a runner runs toward the goal line in order to win the prize. The prize cannot be *taken* by the runner; it must be *given* to the runner after he or she has successfully completed the course. (In other words, the runner does not run toward *the prize*— that would result in disqualification.) In the race Paul has in mind, the prize is resurrection from the dead (v. 11). This is something he must be given; he cannot claim it.

In order to win the *prize* Paul runs toward the *goal* (vv. 12, 14). The goal is that Paul share in the sufferings of Christ and become like him in his death (v. 10). This is Paul's language for what Jesus refers to

THE JOY OF OBEDIENCE

as "losing your life for my sake and the gospel's." It involves faithful striving for the kingdom of God to the point of death. This is the goal toward which Paul presses, forgetting all that lies behind. Paul is clear that he has not yet finished the race; somehow it might be possible, if he did not press on, that he indeed would not finish.

Remember, Paul is writing to the Philippians. He is their founding apostle. They might be tempted to think, *If anyone has made it, Paul has; he should be able to retire.* But Paul isn't planning to retire: "Not that I have already obtained this or have already reached the goal; but I press on to make it my own." Paul says that forgetting what lies behind and straining forward to what lies ahead are critical to his achieving his goal. We can understand this in the athlete analogy: a runner who stops running and turns around to gaze on the distance he has covered is likely to lose. But what does this image mean for Paul?

Paul says he has had to count all things as loss for the sake of Christ: his zealous persecution of the church, his "righteousness" under the law. We easily understand why Paul had to count those things as loss—they were pre-Christian and in fact were obstacles to faith in Christ. But then he says, "I *regard* everything as loss," using the present continuous tense. What is included in the "everything" that he continues to count as loss? Here Paul means all of his recent past (not just his Pharisee past): his church-planting efforts, his missionary work, all those conversions. Paul must count as loss not just his "righteousness" under the law but also his "righteousness" under the gospel. Not just his Pharisee résumé, but his Christian résumé as well.

Why would Paul have to count these good things as loss? I imagine it would be tempting for him, at this point in his life, to relax, to rest on his laurels. We get that image from the ancients, who placed laurel wreaths on the heads of victorious warriors or athletes. So the only way to rest on your laurels is to have completed your race, and Paul says that he hasn't completed his race yet. He has no laurels to rest on.

If anyone had had reason to stop pressing on, it would have been Paul. Yet Paul knows he can win the prize only if he finishes the race by dying in obedience to Jesus. He must continue to strive for the kingdom of God, not stopping until he has literally lost his life for the sake of the gospel, so as to receive it back in the resurrection of the dead. He must count as loss even the good that he has done to advance the gospel, lest it become a snare for him, a point of pride, a subtle means to complacency, preventing him from completing his race.

As for Paul, so for us. As far as we have come in obedience to Jesus, as much as we have learned about discipleship, as long as we have been following Jesus—it will all be for nothing if we do not persevere to the end. Paul tells us to view life the way he does: "Let those of us then who are mature be of the same mind; and if you think differently about anything, this too God will reveal to you. Only let us hold fast to what we have attained" (vv. 15-16).

Paul wants us to think about life as a race, and to press on, running toward the goal for the sake of the prize. But we need to understand how we may be tempted to stop running the race.

The Faces of Disobedience

Paul's urgency in Philippians is rooted in his awareness of the very real possibility that people who begin as disciples may turn away from the path of discipleship. A couple of verses after the end of the passage we've examined, he says, "For many live as enemies of the cross of Christ; I have often told you of them, and now I tell you even with tears" (Philippians 3:18).

Paul isn't telling the Philippians that there are many non-Christians or anti-Christians out there—that's not news. He's telling the Philippians that some people who used to be partners and Christian friends *now* live as enemies—they have repudiated the faith. That is why Paul thinks of them *with tears*. These are people who meant a great deal to Paul and who now oppose him or the gospel message. (See also 2 Timothy 4:10, 14.)

Many friends have told me that the person who was instrumental in their conversion is no longer walking as a Christian. Sometimes it was a youth worker, sometimes a high-school friend or teacher, sometimes a college roommate. But in each case, those who were formerly so committed to their faith eventually found reasons to give it up.

I myself know a number of people who followed Jesus faithfully while in college but hit a snag somewhere afterward and today live as enemies of the cross of Christ. Probably you know people like this as well. We pray for these friends. I also know people who, like the prodigal son, left the care of their loving Father God but then came to their senses and have returned to God. We thank God for his taking hold of his own when they are ready to let go of him.

The reality is that we face many temptations not to press on in the life of faith. I want to identify four different ways we can miss out on the best God wants for each of us who have begun to follow him. I will discuss the four "faces of disobedience" in order of decreasing seriousness and increasing subtlety and likelihood. Jesus, Paul and other New Testament authors all warned their audiences that not all who begin the process of discipleship complete it. My hope is that by identifying faces of disobedience, we can better mark out the path of faithful obedience—that hard, narrow road that leads to life.

Repudiation. We may not think it likely that we will repudiate and outwardly reject the faith within five years, but obviously it could happen. Much of the material in this book is designed to make that possibility less likely. Maintaining active involvement in a meaningful Christian community centered in a Bible-based church will likely give the accountability we need to keep on track. But if we think we are immune to the temptation to repudiation, we are actually more vulnerable to it.

Perhaps surprisingly, repudiation of the faith doesn't usually come about because the theological or philosophical foundations of the faith have been shattered through intellectual challenge. Rather, rejection of the faith often comes about when there is a clash of wills: mine and God's. People leave God when they want to sleep with their girlfriend or marry a non-Christian. They leave God out of a desire to fit in to a non-Christian peer group. Or people leave God because of some promise they think he made to them and then broke—like allowing a loved one to die or suffer tragedy.

Again, the point isn't to dwell on the dismal possibility that we might end our lives in rejection of God, but to acknowledge, as Paul did, that since it *is* a possibility, we want to run the race to the end. We want to put ourselves in the place where we have the best shot at perseverance. This involves all the faithful choices I have talked about since chapter one: rejecting the kingdom of the world and embracing the culture of the kingdom of God, participating in the body of Christ, losing our lives for Christ's sake and the gospel's.

Compromise. OK, so perhaps repudiation of the faith is not too likely, at least for you who are motivated enough to get all the way to the last chapter of a book on discipleship. But a more likely "face of disobedience" is compromise. Not outright repudiation. Not a rejection of the tenets of the faith. Not a denial of the deity of Jesus or of the authority of Scripture. Just a whittling away, an erosion over time of convictions gained about God and our practical obedience to him.

Jesus tells the familiar story of the sower and the soils in Mark 4. Perhaps you have heard this story before and sought to identify with the good soil, hearing and accepting Jesus' teachings and responding to them in the obedience of faith. But let's face it: it may be that you just haven't seriously tangled yet with "the cares of the world, and the lure of wealth, and the desire for other things" (Mark 4:19). (Sounds like graduation from college to me . . .) Perhaps these weeds have yet to come in and choke the Word. How would you know?

Paul warns the Philippians of those "whose minds are set on earthly things" in contrast to those of us whose "citizenship is in heaven." Jesus warns us of those who would try to please two masters. Where is your loyalty: in the world or in God's kingdom? If it is difficult to tell, look at your schedule, your money and your relationships. Are these directed toward the purposes of the kingdom or toward trying to fit in to the world? As you leave college, are you tempted to revise your own hopes for your relationship with God in view of the reality of the "real world"?

One area of potential compromise is in the business world. Paul warns, "Do not be mismatched with unbelievers. For what partnership is there between righteousness and lawlessness? Or what fellowship is there between light and darkness?" (2 Corinthians 6:14). (This is often taken as a prohibition of Christians marrying non-Christians. While it certainly applies, that is probably not the intended application.) It is easy to become mismatched with nonbelievers, especially in business. While I don't think this means we should never work for non-Christians, it does present a warning. When we are hired by someone, we make ourselves tools toward the accomplishment of our employer's goals. (Rarely will people hire us in order to satisfy our goals and desires. That may be a byproduct, but it is not their purpose.) Sometimes their goals aren't antithetical to God's goals. But often the motivation and the ends pursued sound more like "the lure of wealth, and the desire for other things" than like striving for the kingdom. While it's possible to be faithful to the job we were hired to do without falling prey to these motivations, that may make us less than the best company worker. In order to succeed in such an environment, we are tempted to compromise.

In many areas of our lives we're tempted to compromise as we face the imagined cost of faithfulness in an unfaithful world. Of course, ultimately it is faithlessness that is costly, but in the short term things look different. Celibacy before marriage and faithfulness in marriage seem costly in a culture committed to immediate and total gratification of sexual desire. (AIDS, divorce, abortion and sexual violence are some of the long-term costs of our culture's practices.) Choices to serve others and spend your life directing them toward God mean taking on their pain and struggle as your own. When we focus on any of these short-term costs and forget the long-term rewards, we can be tempted to lose heart. Simply seeing the prosperity of those who don't acknowledge God can raise doubts that cause us to compromise.

Psalm 73 is the story of someone who "almost slipped" while seeing the success of pagans who don't acknowledge God. And we battle compromise the way the psalmist did: by regaining a true vision of reality. The psalmist writes:

But when I thought how to understand this [the success
of the wicked],

it seemed to me a wearisome task,
until I went into the sanctuary of God;
then I perceived their end. (Psalm 73:16-17)

The psalmist's vision was restored as he moved from an envious, self-pitying reflection on his circumstances and those of others to a worshipful reflection on the character and work of the Lord God. Worship, Scripture study, and the help and accountability of partners all can help us see through the deception of the world and perceive reality clearly. An accurate vision of reality promotes motivated obedience.

The psalmist gets off track when he takes his eyes off God and begins to look around at others and their lack of faithfulness. And we can get into trouble by comparing our lives to the lives of other Christians. If they are not as far along in their discipleship, we can begin to feel proud of the choices we have made, or we may resent and envy the choices they have made. If we decide to settle for what other Christians are doing, the result may be compromise.

For some people a certain way of life may involve incredible faith in God, while for us the same lifestyle would be compromise. Different people will be called to live out the gospel differently, based on their experiences and gifts. We will meet people who have not been exposed to what we've received from Scripture but who are living faithfully to what they've received. They are taking steps of obedience, trusting God in their work and church commitment; they are involved in ministry.

Both of my parents, for example, became committed Christians after their college years. They are living faithful lives, and while I was growing up they gave me a great spiritual heritage, the foundation of my current discipleship. I love them. They are generous, hospitable people and inspiring Christians. But comfort, convenience and privacy are more important to them than they are to me. I have often suggested, only half in jest, that they sell their house, give the money to missions and move in with another couple in their church whose children are also all grown up. My parents appreciate my choice to live in community, but for them it would be unthinkable.

Much of the difference between us is a difference in our experience of Christian discipleship. We each have responded in faithful ways to God's call. Yet if I were to live like my parents, it would be spiritual compromise for me. And for me to judge them and say that they must follow Jesus the way I do would be wrong as well. They are running their race and are faithful in it. I am running my race, on a different track. I pray that I may be as faithful over the years as they have been.

This is not a Christian relativism ("what's right for me may not be what's right for you") but simply a recognition that we are not accepted by our actions but by our response in faith to the word we have received. The thief on the cross and Peter the apostle were saved in exactly the same way, according to the same standard: they both responded in faith to the word that they heard. This has several implications for us:

☐ We cannot judge people by the word that *we* have received.

☐ We cannot assume that the specific call God places on our lives is for everyone. Indeed, in Scripture we see a diversity of faithful ways to respond to God.

☐ We must not resent other Christians because they have things we don't. To the extent God has given those things as gifts, they should be grateful. We should be grateful for God's generosity to us, which a moment's reflection will reveal. (In Matthew 20:15 Jesus warns against resenting God because of his generosity to others.)

☐ We must not judge ourselves by the standards of others. In order to finish the race, we look toward the finish line, not toward those in the other lanes.

The race analogy falls short in one key respect. In the Olympics only one runner gets the gold medal. But in the race Paul speaks of, everyone who presses on to the end wins the prize. "Let those of us then who are mature be of the same mind. Only let us hold fast to what we have attained." No compromise.

Complacency. Complacency is perhaps the most dangerous face of disobedience, because it is the most subtle. In five years a small percentage of your college Christian friends may have repudiated the faith. Perhaps a slightly higher percentage may have compromised in key decisions. But we can easily imagine that in five years half of your friends from your Christian fellowship or church group will be living complacent lives, satisfied with the level of "radicalness" or commitment they have achieved, and not moving on. Not necessarily sliding back, just holding steady. They don't start running backwards; they just stop, take a look back and relax. Take a stretch in the infield. Watch the rest of the race.

This is the heart of what Paul is warning about. Think of it, this is Paul the apostle. In any five years of his Christian life he accomplished more than any of us do in a lifetime. So what if the last ten years of his life he spent watching TV and doing crossword puzzles? We want to say, "Paul, chill out, man, you've made it." We'd give him a gold watch and let him relax and enjoy life.

But it's important to forget what lies behind and continue to venture into new areas of trust and dependence on God. It doesn't matter if we are giving 25 percent of our income, living in economic community and heavily involved in our church. We must forget what lies behind, not thinking about how great or how radical we are, and continue to press on to what lies ahead.

Just a word about forgetting. Paul says he forgets what lies behind, but in the Old Testament God's people are told to remember.[1] What's the difference?

When the people of Israel are told to remember, what they are to remember is the faithfulness of God, not their own noble or righteous acts. So when we look back on our lives, we are not meant to see the list of wonderful choices we have made for God, but the markers and remembrances of God's faithful presence in our lives. We look back and remember, not to firm up our fragile egos but to enlarge our recognition of God's glory, faithfulness and grace. As we remember, our attitude should be gratitude, not pride.

So Paul's command to us to join him in forgetting what lies behind and God's command to the people of Israel to remember are two sides of the same coin—we forget what we have done, we remember what God has done, and both spur us on to continue in the race and press on, without compromise, without complacency, eager to reach the goal for the sake of the prize.

Joylessness. Prolonged joylessness is the fourth face of disobedience—

"Wait a minute. Are you saying that even though we don't repudiate the faith, compromise our values, or remain complacent, we can still be living disobediently simply by being joyless? Is joylessness really a face of disobedience?"

Paul begins Philippians 3 with the words "Rejoice in the Lord." Let's examine both parts of that.

☐ "Rejoice": Paul challenges his readers: don't be bitter, don't resent the choices you've made. Others will look as if they are doing better, but think about the long run. Rejoice!

☐ "In the Lord": of all the things in Paul's life, only one thing he counted as gain: Christ and becoming like him. We could choose to rejoice in many different parts of our lives, but we are to rejoice in the Lord. Not in our achievements, not in our college degree, not even in our Christian accomplishments. "Rejoice in the Lord."

Paul challenges the Philippians toward joy.

The fact is that prolonged joylessness *is* a sign of disobedience.[2] It is evidence of a lack of faith in God to provide and guide, to care for us as his Word promises. If we don't experience God's love for us, then how can we be gladly growing toward him? How can we minister effectively to others in his name and with his resources? Instead we will grow to resent God throughout the process. Or simply be satisfied with less than joy.

Have you ever thought of joylessness as sin? By *joy* I don't mean a light, fluffy happiness. If we experience joylessness, there is usually something we need to repent of. We may need to repent of the idolatry of the thing we don't have. We may need to repent of our insecurity regarding the thing we do have. We may need to repent of our attitudes toward God, who hasn't produced answers to our prayers in the way we thought he should.

When our hope is not in God, our hope will often disappoint and leave us joyless. The solution is not to find a different temporal object of hope (a new, better job or a more sympathetic boyfriend, for example) but to repent of placing our hope anywhere but in God. Many misplaced affections can rob us of joy. But we can experience a consistent contentment, a deep, abiding joy. We want to be people who are not satisfied with less than joy.

Dissatisfied Contentment

How do we do this? Paul discovered a secret:

> Not that I am referring to being in need; for I have learned to be content with whatever I have. I know what it is to have little, and I know what it is to have plenty. In any and all circumstances I have learned the secret of being well-fed and of going hungry, of having plenty and of being in need. I can do all things through him who strengthens me. (Philippians 4:11-13)

Consider these contrasting images:

☐ a runner, fixed on the goal, driven to complete the race, completely single-minded in pursuit of his stated objective

☐ a man at peace, content with his life and anything that comes his way, able to rejoice in abundance but content in the face of privation and suffering

In the last half of Paul's letter to the Philippians, he uses both of these images to describe himself.

This is Paul's ethic of "dissatisfied contentment."[3] Paul is dissatisfied, not complacent, always moving forward, yet he experiences deep contentment. This dissatisfaction is not a restlessness of spirit, of a person moping about wondering what his life is for. This dissatisfaction is one of motion: he moves forward out of deep inner motivation to draw ever nearer to his Lord Jesus, but the abiding emotion is joy. "Rejoice in the Lord always!" (Philippians 4:4).

Paul is content, but never satisfied; always pressing on, but always rejoicing.

We are too often the exact opposite of Paul. We experience a "satisfied discontent," a complacency of spirit that leads to inertia and stagnation, coupled with an inability to experience joy or deep contentment. We are not dissatisfied enough to press on toward the goal, but we are not content with our lot either. The world says, "If I only had _____, then I'd be happy." Fill in the blank however you want: more money, a boyfriend, better sex, more recognition at work, more free time, an opportunity to travel. The world says, "The right mixture of circumstances and material comforts is the key to contentment." Paul says that the secret of contentment and joy has nothing to do with things and circumstances ("I know what it is to have little, and I know what it is to have plenty"). In fact this must be true, because circumstances change like the weather, but contentment implies an abiding joy, a fundamental condition not subject to hourly updates. Paul's secret lies in valuing the things that God values, striving for his kingdom, living in his will. He can indeed do all things God has called him to do through the empowerment of God's Spirit.

We want to live like Paul did and to learn, over time, his precious secret. We want to press on toward the goal but to experience peace and contentment in the process.

Go for It!

Jesus tells two stories of people who took the plunge and went for it:

> The kingdom of heaven is like treasure hidden in a field, which someone found and hid; then in his joy he goes and sells all that he has and buys that field.
>
> Again, the kingdom of heaven is like a merchant in search of fine pearls; on finding one pearl of great value, he went and sold all that he had and bought it. (Matthew 13:44-46)

Jesus communicates deep truth with an economy of words in these short but powerful parables. The first man, probably a day laborer working in a field, is not particularly looking for anything when he comes across the treasure. In order to own the treasure (rather than simply steal it), he scrapes together his life savings, liquidates all assets and purchases the land in which the treasure is hidden (unbeknownst to the seller). The second man is not a casual laborer but a middle-class merchant, an expert in pearls. He has been looking for fine pearls, but he never expected to find anything quite like *the* pearl, the end of his search. He liquidates his entire collection in order to purchase this single pearl.

In these two simple stories Jesus summarizes the experience of all people who have encountered God. Some spend years looking for him; others bump into him with no prior awareness of their need for him. But both kinds of people respond in the same way: they go and sell all they have in order to acquire the supremely valuable.

This story is compelling because of the ultimate worth of what is obtained in the bargain. Yes, both men must go and sell all they own. In order to acquire the treasure they must part with everything. They can hold nothing back. But this seems to them merely a minor detail—what is crucial is that what is purchased is worth far more than its cost. Clearly it's not an even trade. This explains their attitude in the process: joy.

When we bring our lives to God, we too can hold nothing back. We embark on a lifelong process of selling all, of losing our lives for Christ's sake and the gospel's. The "obedience of faith" (Romans 1:5) involves sacrifices like those the laborer made to purchase the field and the merchant made to acquire the pearl. But in a real sense, no sacrifices are ever made. It is no "sacrifice" to trade away decaying things of temporary value to obtain the thing that never loses its supreme value. When we see the transaction with the eyes of faith, the only possible response is joy. Deep, abiding joy. The kind of joy Jesus had. The joy he wants for us.

When Jesus came onto the scene in Galilee, he preached, "The time is fulfilled, and the kingdom of God has come near; repent, and believe in the good news" (Mark 1:15). This is the summary of the good news: God's King is finally on center stage, intervening in this world. He comes with all the authority, wisdom and power of God, yet he comes as a servant to call people to join the kingdom and swear allegiance to himself, the Servant-King.

Striving for the kingdom of God is a sure thing—because the outcome is assured: God's kingdom is indeed coming! We are not betting on a long shot. We are not joining the side likely to lose. This is not some obscure, utopian solve-the-world's-problems campaign. The kingdom of God is a sure thing. Jesus' resurrection proved that.

What's more, *striving for the kingdom of God is a good thing*. Not only is the outcome assured, but the process yields satisfaction of the deepest desires of our hearts: life, security, greatness, purpose, joy. The King of the kingdom is God's King, God's good, righteous, loving Servant-King, who knows us like a shepherd knows his sheep, and who will lead us and guide us to green pastures and cool, clear water.

So go for it! Press on toward the goal, counting as loss all that lies behind. Want even more than you have yet experienced in your relationship with God and in your experience of the body of Christ. Strain forward, press on, finish the race. And in the process lay aside all attachments that would keep you from knowing the joy Jesus desires for you. Experience the abiding joy, peace and contentment of being in the care of God.

■ For Reflection
The Faces of Disobedience
☐ We battle complacency by continually taking steps forward in our discipleship. What steps have you taken recently?
☐ Security breeds complacency. Is your security in God and his people? Does that security inspire you to take faithful risks or keep you from rocking the boat?
☐ What faith-inspired risks have you taken recently?

Dissatisfied Contentment
☐ Joy is not a minute-by-minute monitor of our spiritual progress. Day to day it isn't necessarily to be our focus. But reflecting back over time, ask yourself: Do I experience a fundamental contentment?
☐ What (in me, not in my circumstances) needs to change so that I can experience joy?
☐ What does repentance mean for me at this point?

For Further Reading
Clinton, J. Robert. *The Making of a Leader.* Colorado Springs: NavPress, 1988. This book addresses the process God uses to make leaders over a lifetime. It is helpful to give a long-term perspective on God's work in a person's life.

Notes and Acknowledgments

I have been involved in ministry to students since I was one myself, and I have learned much from many people. Unfortunately, most of that cannot be cited or referenced, since the learning happened informally or nonformally, not through written material. I am grateful for my InterVarsity Christian Fellowship staff experience, the training I received and multiple opportunities to teach.

The manuscript of this book went through several revisions, and I received helpful feedback from a number of people who care about the concerns the book raises as much as I do. My current and former IVCF supervisors, Doug Whallon and John Ratichek, have both been very helpful and supportive. John's clarifying feedback on chapter four was especially helpful. Encouragement and insight also came from other IVCF staff from around the United States: Al Anderson, Randy Bare, Steve Barr, Barbara Boyd, Robbie Castleman, Kathy Cooper, Bill Cutler, Gary Deddo, Terry Erickson, Bob Grahmann, Bobby Gross, John Hochevar, Paul Hughes, David Lamb, Geri Rodman, Lou Soiles, Pete Sommer, Paul Sorrentino, Steve Stuckey, Steve Tuttle and Alex Van Riesen. A few other people have also given me good feedback: Elisa Bosley, Shane Chao, Lauren and Tyson Cobb, Nikolay Mak, Melinda Melone, Doug Selph and Nancy Washington. Beyond those mentioned, dozens of alumni have contributed by filling out questionnaires designed to help me better understand the concerns and issues facing recent alumni. John Alexander, founding editor of *The Other Side* and author of *The Secular Squeeze,* provided helpful early editing and critical suggestions. My wife, Lisa, was my true partner in this project and in the lifestyle it speaks of, and has contributed to both the ideas and their presentation throughout.

Chapter 1: What Do You Expect?
I am indebted for much of this material to Greg Read, IVCF staff at Stanford

during my undergraduate days there and now an associate pastor of Vineyard Christian Fellowship, San Francisco. His emphasis on repentance and his gift of analysis of the culture laid the foundation for the specific challenges I present here.

[1]Real median income of U.S. families, from 1973 to 1990, showed growing disparity between those under age thirty and those over sixty-five. Average income for families headed by someone over sixty-five increased nearly 40 percent in real terms, while average income for families headed by someone under age thirty decreased by 16 percent during those same years. In previous decades the increases in income had been spread fairly equally across age brackets. Also, in this same time span the poverty rate for families with children where the family head was under thirty years old doubled, from 16 percent to 33 percent, while poverty rates for families whose head was over thirty grew only a few percentage points, from 9 percent to 12 percent. Source: U.S. Bureau of the Census, cited in Neil Howe and Bill Strauss, *13th Gen: Abort, Retry, Ignore, Fail?* (New York: Vintage, 1993), pp. 94-95.

[2]Acts 4:19-20; 5:19-29. While we are always supposed to *honor* authorities, we are not necessarily supposed to *obey* them, if God's call comes first. This is true of parents and governing authorities. Jesus' remarks in Mark 3:33-35; 10:29-30; and Luke 9:59-60; 14:26 make it clear that his authority and claim on the lives of his disciples is higher than that of parents.

Chapter 2: The King and the Kingdom

I am indebted to the strong tradition of emphasizing the lordship of Christ throughout IVCF. The structure of this book in general, and the first two chapters specifically, reflects the structure of one of IVCF's foundational training programs, Bible & Life.

Chapter 3: Productivity and Prayer

This chapter reflects the emphasis and wisdom of Doug Gregg, IVCF staff and Presbyterian pastor in Los Angeles. His teaching has spurred my own prayer life forward.

[1]S. D. Gordon, *Quiet Talks on Prayer* (New York: Revell, 1941), p. 18.

[2]Charles Hummel, *Tyranny of the Urgent* (Downers Grove, Ill.: InterVarsity Press, 1967). A revised edition of this booklet was issued by IVP in 1994.

Chapter 4: Meaningless Work and Fruitful Labor

I am grateful for Tom Sine's challenging book *The Mustard Seed Conspiracy* (Waco, Tex.: Word, 1981) for helping to orient me to a dynamic view of vocation in the kingdom of God. I am also grateful for several excellent insights from Kevin Rhodes, a teaching elder in a church in Boulder, Colorado.

[1]"From 1975 to 1988, the proportion of high school seniors who believed that 'to me, work is nothing more than making a living' rose from 19 to 25 percent." From "Monitoring the Future: Questionnaire Responses from the Nation's High School Seniors" (Ann Arbor: University of Michigan, 1975-1988), cited in Neil Howe and Bill Strauss, *13th Gen: Abort, Retry, Ignore, Fail?* (New York: Vintage, 1993), p. 107.

[2]John A. Bernbaum and Simon M. Steer, *Why Work? Careers and Employment in Biblical Perspective* (Grand Rapids, Mich.: Baker Book House, 1986); see the discussion on pp. 34-42.

[3]John Perkins, *A Quiet Revolution* (Waco, Tex.: Word, 1976), pp. 33-34, cited in Sine, *Mustard Seed Conspiracy,* pp. 140-41.

[4]I am indebted to Sine, *Mustard Seed Conspiracy,* especially the discussion on page 140, for turning the common question around.

Chapter 5: Community After College

My understanding of community has grown over many years and comes from many sources. I would like to acknowledge Church of the Sojourners in San Francisco for the clarity of its call to community and its challenge to me.

[1]For example, the Sermon on the Mount (Matthew 5—7) and the Upper Room discourse (John 13—17). Furthermore, most of the parables of the kingdom invite individual participation in what is fundamentally a communal experience: a party, a banquet, a wedding feast. Individuals must leave behind family, but only to enter into a much larger family.

[2]Jesus' promises of answered prayer (Matthew 7:7-11; Mark 11:22-24; Luke 11:5-13; John 15:7) are given most fundamentally to the gathered community of believers. These are not "health and wealth" promises, but rather promises that the community of God has access to the resources of God to meet legitimate needs of the people and to pursue the purposes of the kingdom.

[3]Gerhard Lohfink, *Jesus and Community* (Philadelphia: Fortress, 1984), pp. 157-63.

[4]Home ownership by those under twenty-five years of age decreased by over 30 percent between 1973 and 1990, according to the Joint Center for Housing Studies of Harvard University. This study was cited by Neil Howe and Bill Strauss, *13th Gen: Abort, Retry, Ignore, Fail?* (New York: Vintage, 1993), p. 95.

[5]Robert Bellah et al., *Habits of the Heart* (New York: Harper & Row, 1985), p. 115.

[6]Here Paul is speaking about the body of Christ, understood as the church. I have been speaking of a *community*, a word that I am using to refer to what

might be a church or merely a subset of a church. My understanding is that
Paul's hope for the functioning church applies to any functioning community within a church. The next chapter will examine Paul's vision of the
church and our participation in it more fully.

[7]Obviously many communities change over time because people move away.
There can be good ways for this to happen and bad or destructive ways. Our
aim is community life that can endure through changes as people come and
go, and that people who leave have good reasons to leave, not simply that
they are giving up on community.

[8]Twelve-step programs offer the meaningful accountability needed to help
people take these steps. Christian community should do so as well.

[9]For example, a high-school sports team could be viewed as a clique with a
purpose or vision. It is much less likely to fall apart.

Chapter 6: Strategies for Church Involvement

I am grateful to have been involved in a couple of healthy and growing
churches since college, most recently a Conservative Baptist church in Cam-
bridge. I was challenged early on in my thinking on the church by several
of Howard Snyder's books (*The Problem of Wineskins* [Downers Grove, Ill.:
InterVarsity Press, 1975], *The Community of the King* [Downers Grove, Ill.:
InterVarsity Press, 1977], *Liberating the Church* [Downers Grove, Ill.: InterVarsity Press, 1983]). For the original exegesis of Acts 26 I am indebted again to
Greg Read.

[1]Vernard Eller, *The Outward Bound* (Grand Rapids, Mich.: Eerdmans, 1980),
pp. 12-13.

[2]Avery Dulles, *Models of the Church* (New York: Doubleday, 1974), p. 27, cited
in Snyder, *Community of the King*, p. 38.

[3]See, for example, Snyder, *The Problem of Wineskins*.

Chapter 7: A Mobilized Lifestyle for the Kingdom

[1]Richard Foster, *Celebration of Discipline* (San Francisco: Harper & Row, 1978),
p. 70.

[2]A great place to begin to read about racial reconciliation is Spencer Perkins
and Chris Rice, *More Than Equals: Racial Healing for the Sake of the Gospel*
(Downers Grove, Ill.: InterVarsity Press, 1993).

Chapter 8: Embracing a Lifestyle of Ministry

[1]For the disciples and the people of Jesus' day, relatives, including parents,
siblings and kids, formed the social security system, the safety net that pro-
tected individuals from starvation and poverty. The larger this net was, the

more security one felt. Jesus says to his disciples, "I know you have left behind your social security net. Don't worry, because the network of relationships you have entered into will be a hundred times larger. You will have family, fields and houses far beyond your needs."

Chapter 10: The Joy of Obedience

I am indebted to Daniel Fuller and John Piper for my understanding of the proper connection between joy and obedience. Piper's *Desiring God* (Portland, Ore.: Multnomah Press, 1986) and Fuller's *The Unity of the Bible* (Grand Rapids, Mich.: Zondervan, 1992) provide a wealth of insight into this connection and its application in the life of a Christian. The title of the chapter and some of the foundational insights again derive from Greg Read.

[1]See Exodus 13:3: "Moses said to the people, 'Remember this day on which you came out of Egypt, out of the house of slavery, because the LORD brought you out from there by strength of hand; no leavened bread shall be eaten.' " The command to remember is also found in Deuteronomy 5:15; 7:18; 8:18; 16:3, among other places.

[2]Both Jesus and Paul command us to rejoice. Jesus, in the Sermon on the Mount, calls us to "rejoice and be glad" even in the face of persecution (Matthew 5:12).

[3]This phrase was coined by John Piper; see "Holy Hedonism," *His*, November 1981.